Franklin Field Saturdays

Celebrating 65 Years of Penn Football in the Ivy League

1956-2021

by Ted Gilmore

This book is dedicated to all Penn football players, past and present, for all of the thrills, excitement and memories they have provided at Franklin Field for 125 seasons.

Acknowledgements

This book would not have been possible without the invaluable assistance and encouragement of the following people, whom I will never be able to thank enough:

- Lisbeth Willis, Penn's Director of Classes & Reunions, Penn Alumni, who put me in contact with all of the right people to get this project started, including Barrett Freedlander and Dan Rottenberg.
- Barrett Freedlander, Member of the Penn Football Board, who not only assisted me in contacting several key members of the Penn football family (including head coach Ray Priore), but who also wrote the marvelous Foreword to this book. I also appreciate his candor and guidance throughout this whole process.
- Dan Rottenberg, Author of "Fight on Pennsylvania" (*the* definitive history of Penn football), whose advice was "spot on," and whose encouragement was inspirational.
- Mike Mahoney, Penn's Sports Information Director, who granted me permission to use any and all materials I needed from the Penn Athletics website.
- Christine Knooren, *Daily Pennsylvanian* Office Manager, who did the same for me re the *DP's* Archives.
- Ray Priore, Penn Head Football Coach, who read several sample chapters" of the proposed book, and thereafter gave his "blessing" for it, and put me in touch with:
- Nick Morris and Gary Vura, former Penn players and current Football Board members, who assisted me in gathering personal written recollections of the games from the players, including:
- Barney Berlinger, Mike Chico, Brandon Copeland, John Doman, Bobby Fallon, Vahe Gregorian, Gavin Hoffman, Fred Levin, Miles Macik, Jim McGeehan,

John McGeehan, Mike Mitchell, Jake Perskie and Terrance Stokes. All of your stories were great, guys. And an additional thank you goes to Jake Perskie for the photo he included with his story.
- Susie Perloff, who knew more about football than she realized.
- Sarah Stupak, my amazing granddaughter, whose technical assistance in the initial stages of this project helped to move it from just an idea to a real possibility.
- Glenn Pudelka, Esq., my ever-patient nephew, for answering any legal questions I had.
- George Sucher, my great friend, who provided me with valuable information on how to structure a book such as this one.
- Butch Heine and Pete Bauer – two more great friends, who, although not Penn alums, should be honorary ones, for all of the games they have attended with me over the years. Go Quakers, you two!
- Holly and Brian, my two awesome children, for putting up with my Penn fanaticism – hope I didn't embarrass you too much, kids. (See Brian's account of the '82 Harvard game on page 105).
- Marygrace (last but not least), my beloved wife of 50 years, who gave me the space and encouragement to complete this project, with nary a word of complaint throughout.

Thank you dear, for the above, and also for *your* technical assistance (when needed) as well.

Copyright © 2021 by Ted Gilmore
All rights reserved. No part of this book may be used or reproduced in any manner whatsoever without written permission, except in the case of brief quotations embodied in critical articles or reviews.

Cover Design: Dwayne Booth

Published 2021 by Shorehouse Books
Printed in the United States of America

ISBN-13: 978-1-7372746-3-6

Table of Contents

Introduction	1
Foreword – Barrett Freedlander	3
Prologue: October 6, 1956	5
1. A League of Their Own 1956	7
2. Man Bites Dog 1957	11
3. New Rules 1958	14
4. Team of Destiny? 1959	18
5. In the Driver's Seat 1959	21
6. Once Upon a Cold Thanksgiving Day 1959	24
7. Who Loves Harvard? 1963	29
8. We Got Our Kicks 1965	35
9. Lion Taming 1965	38
10. Tiger Taming 1968	41
11. Scout's Honor 1968	45
12. This Guy's the 3rd Stringer? 1969	48
13. So Close 1970	52
14. Son of So Close 1971	56
15. Shue Fit 1972	59
16. Riding the Wave 1972	62
17. What Might Have Been 1972	65
18. Homecoming Heartbreaker 1973	71
19. Beep Beep 1973	75
20. Tiger Trap 1974	78
21. Like They Had Won the Rose Bowl 1975	81
22. Tiger Kings 1977	84
23. Finally 1980	87
24. Vura to Hall 1981	90
25. Curtain Call 1982	94
26. The Miracle on 33rd Street 1982	99
27. Butler Didn't Do It 1983	106
28. Back-to-Back 1983	109
29. Three in a Row 1984	113
30. Doctor Who 1985	117
31. Four in a Row 1985	120
32. (On the Way to) Five in a Row 1986	124
33. No Taunting, Please 1987	127

34.	Sweet Revenge 1988	131
35.	Ivies on Notice 1992	135
36.	Youth Must Be Served 1993	138
37.	The ~~Keith Elias~~ Terrance Stokes Game 1993	143
38.	The 100th Meeting 1993	149
39.	One Shining Moment 1994	153
40.	Changing of the Guard 1995	160
41.	Victory in the Gloamin' 1997	163
42.	Champs Once Again 1998	167
43.	The Comeback 2000	170
44.	The Comeback, Part *Deux* 2000	174
45.	"GameDay" 2002	178
46.	All's Well That Ends Well 2003	183
47.	Castles in the Air 2003	185
48.	The Fumble 2004	190
49.	*Déjà vu* All Over Again 2007	195
50.	Home Cooking on Homecoming 2009	198
51.	"We're Baack" 2009	201
52.	Introducing "Billy Ball" 2010	204
53.	Another Championship 2010	207
54.	Great Scott 2012	210
55.	Sweet Sixteenth 2012	213
56.	Last Man Standing 2013	218
57.	Missing the Point 2013	221
58.	Block That Kick, Donald 2015	224
59.	Quick Work 2015	227
60.	Elementary 2016	230
61.	The Drive 2016	233
62.	Will to Win 2017	236
63.	The Greatest 2017	240
64.	Nail-Biter 2019	244
65.	Razzle Dazzle 2019	247
	Wait 'Till Next Year 2020	250
	Bibliography/Sources	252

Ted Gilmore

Introduction

As part of a three-generation University of Pennsylvania family, I have attended football games at Franklin Field since 1957. My first game was that season's contest against Dartmouth. I was hooked for life the moment I entered the historic stadium. Sixty-three years later, in 2020, the coronavirus caused the cancellation of the entire football season, at Penn and many other colleges across the country. Franklin Field, both literally and metaphorically empty, left a gaping hole that I needed to fill for myself. Hence, this book.

This book is not a treatise on the history of Penn football - Dan Rottenberg's marvelous 1985 book "Fight On, Pennsylvania" is the definitive work on that. What I have gathered here is a compilation of snapshots, narrative and pictorial – a scrapbook, if you will – of 65 memorable Ivy League football games played at Franklin Field since the conference began round-robin play in 1956. It is meant to celebrate the 65th anniversary - 1956 to 2021 – of Penn football in the Ivy League. It also pays homage to the glory and majesty of the grand stadium at 33rd and Spruce Streets in Philadelphia, the oldest college football stadium in the United States. Built for football 126 years ago, there is still no better place to watch a football game than Franklin Field. On game days, with the stadium's double deck bleachers, brick construction and over 100 years of memories, the atmosphere for fans is all-encompassing. And when the old building is empty, one can actually feel the presence of the ghosts of players who have gone before - many, many players, past and present, confirm this.

In my opinion, the story of Penn football in the Ivy League can has two parts:
    1) 1956 – 1980: Before (head coach) Jerry Berndt.
    2) 1981 – present: The Jerry Berndt Years and After.
Part one was a period of solid mediocrity at best. Part two is a period of sustained excellence that continues to this day. The striking contrast between the two parts becomes readily apparent if you read about the games in the chronological order of the chapters.

Note: The materials in the individual game narratives are excerpted with permission from the pages of the *Daily Pennsylvanian Archives* and *the Penn Athletics* website. The original writers of the articles (if known) are cited in the "Sources" pages in the back of this book. I also include compelling personal remembrances that players wrote for me about participating in these games. I selected some games which obviously required inclusion, such as the 1982 contest against Harvard - arguably the most dramatic Penn football game ever played at Franklin Field. For some others, the reason(s) for selection may be slightly more nuanced. Spoiler alerts: A few of the selected games, while truly thrilling, did not end in victory for Penn. An even smaller number of games did not occur on a Saturday. No doubt some readers will wish I had included or excluded particular games, but they will probably agree that all the selected games are memorable in some way. To me, *every* game ever played at Franklin Field is memorable.

I hope that Penn fans everywhere, young and not-so-young, enjoy this book as much as I enjoyed putting it together. Go Quakers!

Ted Gilmore, Class of 1970

2021

Foreword

In 2006, our son informed us that he would be getting married that fall in San Juan, Puerto Rico, to a Penn classmate, of course, on the first weekend in November. Upon realizing that the wedding would conflict with Penn's homecoming football game, he graciously said, "Dad, I will understand if you skip the wedding." I skipped the game.

George Weiss, affectionately called the "team owner" by past and present players, also confronted a conflict between the gridiron and the marital altar. According to the schedule for his wedding, his honeymoon would overlap the start of the Penn football season. His solution was simple: Honeymoon *before* the wedding.

Bill Constantine, a wonderful champion of Penn football during his many years as president of the Penn Football Club, demonstrated his devotion differently: In 2004, when the Quakers played the University of San Diego at the latter's home field, Bill chartered and subsidized the round-trip plane carrying the full team, coaches, administrators, cheerleaders and band. When the plane landed in California, the flight attendant said to Bill, "Those players are really nice kids." That was Bill's reward. Penn won big (61-18), and the following fall, an unusually large number of Californians joined the team.

Into this pantheon of Penn football worshippers – some may come up with less charitable descriptions of us – now steps Ted Gilmore, Class of 1970, whose constancy dates to 1957. For 64 years he rarely missed a Penn football game at Franklin Field.

Recently COVID provided Ted with spare time, an ideal opportunity to immortalize his devotion to Penn football by compiling a book about its most memorable Ivy League home games. His enchantment with the football spectacles at Franklin Field motivated him to convey his joy and appreciation to the players, devoted alumni and fans, and to future generations of same.

Happily Ted reliably selected the right games. Starting with original write-ups by the *Daily Pennsylvanian* and pennathletics.com, Ted adds his own unique perspective as both an historian and an eye witness. He includes reminiscences of many of the warriors whose heroics saved the day. Their accounts of the games add a special quality to this absorbing book.

Dear Reader, I heartily recommend that you read this book from cover to cover. Even if you choose to be more selective, though, you will be delighted with the result.

Barrett Freedlander, Class of 1962

Prologue: October 6, 1956

Penn's entrance into the formal Ivy League conference was somewhat complicated. Here is the short version.

Early in 1954, eight college and university presidents signed the Ivy Group Presidents' Agreement, establishing the formal Ivy League: Penn plus Brown, Columbia, Cornell, Dartmouth, Harvard, Princeton and Yale.

Despite its acceptance into this new league, because it had been playing "big-time" football for almost 80 years, Penn had to overcome the doubts of the other seven schools that it would abide by the new Ivy restrictions, which banned athletic scholarships and spring practice and required that academic authorities control athletic endeavors. Through the lobbying efforts of its athletic director, Jeremiah Ford, Penn convinced the other schools that it would indeed play by Ivy rules.

However, Penn still had one big problem: Round-robin play among the member schools was not to begin until 1956, and Penn had already established its schedules for the 1954 and 1955 seasons.

Thus Penn faced murderous schedules in 1954 and 1955, with opponents including Notre Dame, Penn State, Duke, Army, Navy and California, and would have to play these teams under the above new restrictions. Princeton and Cornell were the only Ivy opponents scheduled for each of the above two seasons. In addition, Penn would be playing under a new head coach, **Steve Sebo**, since coach George Munger had stepped down at the end of the 1953 season. Further complicating matters was the fact that, in 1953 the NCAA rules committee had abolished the two-platoon system.✓ Thus, with no

---

✓ Prior to 1941, virtually all college football players played both offensive and defensive roles. By rule, substitution of players was very restricted. Then, from 1941 through 1952, the National Collegiate Athletic Association (NCAA) established a new set of rules, allowing for *unlimited* player substitutions. However,

spring practice, Sebo had exactly 23 days to convert to single-platooning and install his new offense. The initial results were predictable: the shell-shocked Quakers played a total of 18 games in the 1954 and 1955 seasons and lost Every. Single. One.

Losing the 1956 season opener to Penn State (34-0) brought the streak to 19 games. One week later, the 1st official Ivy League season began. For Penn, that meant a game against Dartmouth at Franklin Field. The curtain was rising on a new epoch for Penn football in particular and Penn sports in general. How would the Quakers compete in this new Ivy League? Would they rise to the top against teams in their own competition class? Or would they continue to lose? Everyone was about to find out.

---

for the 1953 season, the NCAA reversed itself again, requiring the use of a "one-platoon" system and allowing only very limited substitutions. Over the next 11 seasons, the NCAA liberalized these rules, finally totally repealing them in 1964 and again allowing unlimited player substitutions. Thus, teams could now in essence form two platoons, that is, separate offensive and defensive units.

1. A League of Their Own

October 6, 1956 - Penn 14, Dartmouth 7

"Here comes the sun."

Quakers Win 1st Ivy Game, End 19-Game Losing Streak

Penn's **Dick Schafer** *hauls in the winning TD pass from* **Rich Ross**.

> *"Never in my life have we been leading at the end of the 3rd quarter."*
> **Neil Hyland,** Penn running back

A much bedraggled and belittled Penn team, fired up by the stigma of 19 straight defeats and some alleged pre-game remarks by the opposition's coach, picked itself out of the doldrums with a smashing 14-7 victory over Dartmouth at Franklin Field. It was a marvelous debut in the newly-formalized Ivy League, which, per the 1954 Ivy

Franklin Field Saturdays

agreement, "subjugated big-time play in favor of close, keen competition."

The Quakers were now in their own competition class – and it showed, as they finally broke the longest major-college losing streak in the nation. They sent some 15,568 astonished spectators home happy, with the realization that Penn football was reborn in a new world of Ivy League play. Except for the opening few minutes, when Dartmouth scored a quick touchdown, the Quakers were in command virtually the whole way. In prior years, the above score, which put Dartmouth ahead 7-0 at 7:09 of the 1st period, might have left the Red and Blue players demoralized, with thoughts of "here we go again."

Instead, it seemed to fire them up even more, as they marched 74 yards downfield in the next series of plays and tied things up at 11:09 of the same quarter. Seventeen minutes later, Penn showed that this was no fluke, by driving another 72 yards for what turned out to be the winning touchdown. With time running out in the half, end **Dick Schafer** raced behind a drawn-in Dartmouth secondary and pulled in quarterback **Rich Ross**'s perfect 25-yard pass in the end zone, putting the Quakers ahead 14-7.

Dartmouth fought back with a vengeance in the 2nd half, but there was no further scoring by either team. An interception late in the 4th quarter by **Frank Riepl** (who also kicked two extra points) squashed the final Dartmouth threat, and Penn (and Penn fans) celebrated the Quakers' 1st victory in three years.

Score by Quarters					
	1	2	3	4	Total
Dartmouth	7	0	0	0	7
Penn	7	7	0	0	14

Scoring Summary
Dartmouth – Brown 1 run (Palermo kick)
Penn – Hyland 4 run (Riepl kick)
Penn – Schafer 25 pass from Ross (Riepl kick)
Attendance – 15,568

1956: A Good Start
In the Ivy League's inaugural season, Penn finished with a respectable 4-3 league record. The season ended on a sour note however, when the team inexplicably came out flat for the Thanksgiving Day finale at Franklin Field. With the Quakers having a chance to finish with a winning record overall for the 1st time in four years, a previously winless Cornell team thoroughly outplayed them, 20-7. Still, with a solid core of players returning next year, the future looked bright.

A Great Start – Penn (Finally) Wins

*Penn halfback **Neil Hyland** smashes into the end zone for a TD, tying the score at 7-7.*

Jubilant Penn fans celebrate their team's 1st victory in three years.

2. *Man Bites Dog*

November 9, 1957 - Penn 33, Yale 20

"When a dog bites a man, that is not news. But if a man bites a dog, that is news."

Sebo's Men Bite Heavily Favored Bulldogs

The Yale players watch the clock run out, as Penn pulls off a major upset.

On paper, it seemed like a mismatch. The Yale Bulldogs, the defending Ivy League champion at 5-1, with the one loss by a single point, faced the 0-6 Penn Quakers, whose student body was clamoring for the firing of head coach Steve Sebo. Indeed, when Yale jumped out to a 13-0 lead in the 1st quarter, it appeared that the predicted rout was on. Except it wasn't. Before the 1st quarter ended, Penn running back **Bill Young** ran through a giant hole in the Yale line and galloped 62 yards for a touchdown.

Then Penn quarterback **Frank Riepl**, returning from an ankle injury suffered in the season opener against Penn State, sparked the team further by scoring two more touchdowns. One was on an 8-yard dash around right end, and the other on a quarterback sneak from the 1-foot line, after another startling dash – of 57 yards by Bill Young in the 3rd quarter – had put the ball there. For the defense, Penn's **Ray Kelly** made some key defensive tackles, which helped seal the Bulldogs' fate. At one point, Penn was leading by the improbable score of 33-13. A late Yale touchdown made the final score a bit more respectable for the Eli, but, in the end, there was no question as to which was the better team on this Franklin Field Saturday.

Score by Quarters					
	1	2	3	4	**Total**
Yale	13	0	0	7	**20**
Penn	7	6	14	6	**33**

Scoring Summary
Yale – Hallas 2 run (kick failed)
Yale – Winkler 62 pass from Winterbauer (Winterbauer kick)
Penn – Young 62 run (Riepl kick)
Penn – Riepl 8 run (kick failed)
Penn - Riepl 1 run (Riepl kick)
Penn – Koze 6 run (Riepl kick)
Penn – Hanlon 54 run (kick failed)
Yale – Lorch 2 run (Winterbauer kick)
Attendance – 15,319

1957: Riepl Effect

Fans and sports writers expected great things for the Quakers this year. Indeed, when they nearly knocked off Penn State, losing 19-14 in the opener at Franklin Field, expectations rose even higher. However, an ankle injury suffered in that game by star senior quarterback Frank Riepl doomed the Red and Blue. Without Riepl, four close league losses plus a blowout by Navy occurred, and the next thing the Quakers knew, they were 0-6. Riepl finally returned for the above Yale game, and with him Penn easily went 3-0 the rest of the way, leaving Quaker fans pondering what might have been.

Frank Riepl

3. New Rules

October 18, 1958 - Penn 21, Brown 20

"One is the loneliest number that you'll ever do."

Quakers Stop "2-Pointer" to Gain 1st Victory of Season

Penn quarterback Tom Twitmeyer (15) tosses a 2nd-period aerial, as Ed Goodwin (33) holds off an on-rushing Bruin lineman.

Bouncing back after losing two heart-breaking decisions in consecutive games, the Quakers pulled out a thrilling 21-20 victory over Brown in one of the strangest, yet most exciting, games ever seen at Franklin Field. While the opposing backfields fumbled the ball back and forth, 3rd-string Quaker end **Terry Ward** gathered in two touchdown passes from quarterback **Larry Purdy** to win the game in the final period and give the Red and Blue its 1st victory of the season. To add to the excitement, the new 2-point conversion rule determined the outcome.

After a scoreless 1st quarter, at 6:04 of the 2nd, Penn halfback **Dick Koze** electrified the crowd with a 72-yard TD dash from scrimmage. After bursting through a hole in the center of the Bruin line, Koze turned on the speed and outraced the Brown secondary to the end zone, making the score 7-0 Penn.

Following the kick-off, the game became one of turnovers. First Penn's **Jack Hanlon** intercepted a Bruin pass on the Penn 45. Four plays later, Brown blocked a Penn punt and recovered the ball on the Quaker 28. One play later, Hanlon fell on a Brown fumble on the Penn 33, but on the next play Hanlon fumbled a pitch out, and Brown had the ball back on the Penn 29. Purdy, playing defense, secured another Penn interception before the Quakers obliged again by fumbling the elusive pigskin back to the visitors on the Red and Blue's 39. This time, the Bruins ultimately cashed in from one yard out and converted their 2-point attempt to take an 8-7 lead into the locker room. Brown increased its lead to 14-7 early in the 3rd period, going 69 yards in seven plays to score. The Bruins' Paul Choquette, who lived up to his advance notices by grinding out huge hunks of yardage all afternoon, bulled his way over from the 1; however, **Hal Musick** stopped Brown's attempt to add two more points.

Penn took the lead for keeps early in the final period. Purdy threw a 41-yard touchdown pass to Ward, then flipped to **John Terpak** for two more points and a 15-14 lead. **Ron Champion** set up the final Quaker score by intercepting yet another Brown pass at the Bruin 26. Two plays later, sharp-shooting Purdy again zeroed in on Ward, to increase the Quakers lead to 21-14. However, the Brown defense stopped Hanlon short of the goal on a 2-point conversion attempt, and back came the determined Bruins again. An 11-play, 68-yard scoring drive ended with a 2-yard TD plunge by Choquette, and the score now stood at 21-20.

With precious little time on the clock, it all came down to the new 2-point conversion, and Brown lined up to attempt just that. With the game on the line, Penn tackle **Bruce Cummings** heroically stopped a "bull-like charge" of Choquette, writing the end to an exhilarating Franklin Field Saturday.

*Penn linemen **Denny Troychak** and **Skip Couser** stop Brown's Bob Topping on the Penn 3-yard line.*

Score by Quarters					
	1	2	3	4	Total
Brown	0	8	6	6	**20**
Penn	0	7	0	14	**21**

Scoring Summary
Penn -   Koze 72 run (Shaw kick)
Brown -   Barry 1 run (Finney run)
Brown -   Choquette 1 run (run failed)
Penn -   Ward 41 pass from Purdy (Terpak pass from Purdy)
Penn -   Ward 6 pass from Purdy (pass failed)
Brown -   Choquette 2 run (run failed)
Attendance – 16,291

1958: Some Progress Made
Another tough start left the Quakers at 0-3. Following an opening-day loss to Penn State in the final game in that series, Penn suffered two crushingly close losses to top Ivy contenders Dartmouth (13-12) and Princeton (20-14). The Quakers' luck finally turned in the above game against Brown, and surprisingly easy victories over Harvard, Yale and Columbia followed. Once again though, an inexplicably lackluster (19-7) loss to Cornell on Thanksgiving Day thwarted a winning season.

4. Team of Destiny?

October 3, 1959 - Penn 13, Dartmouth 0

"There's something happening here; but what it is ain't exactly clear."

Quakers Now Set Sights on Ivy League Title

*Penn quarterback **Larry Purdy** (16) hands off to **John Terpak** (24), as **Jack Hanlon** (17) and **John Marciano** (53) lead the blocking.*

"This is the most wonderful thing that's ever happened around here. We beat Dartmouth."
Ed Smith, Penn lineman

The sweet smell of success, tinged with the scent of Ivy Championship laurels, threw the undefeated, untied and unscored-upon Penn football team into the Ivy League football limelight. In their 1959 league opener at Franklin Field, the Quakers upset defending champion Dartmouth 13-0. Penn's football renaissance had now shifted into high gear, as coach Steve Sebo's determined, hard-hitting squad totally outplayed the Big Green in an explosive, rough and tumble struggle.

Fred Doelling ran for a touchdown in the 2nd quarter on a 10-yard sweep, and the score remained 7-0 until the closing minutes of the game. After a Dartmouth drive stalled on the Penn 19 with three minutes to play, Doelling scored again from the Dartmouth 45, as **John**

Terpak threw two different blocks to spring him loose. The victory was sealed, and Penn's 1959 season was off to a great start.

Score by Quarters	1	2	3	4	Total
Dartmouth	0	0	0	0	0
Penn	0	7	0	6	13

Scoring Summary
Penn – Doelling 10 run (Shaw kick)
Penn – Doelling 45 run (kick failed)
Attendance - 16,184

Sweet Taste of Victory by William T. Bates, Sports Editor, *Daily Pennsylvanian*
The big hands on the clock on the southwest side of the field indicated that only four minutes remained in the game. Feeling contented that Penn had a 7-point lead at this time, we left our lofty perch high atop the north stands and threaded our way down to the Dartmouth sideline in nothing flat. Johnny Terpak ripped off five yards over left tackle, and the timepiece said that 2:40 remained in the game. "Control the ball," we thought, "and the game is won." Then it happened. Fred Doelling rocketed around the end, and fullback **Jack Hanlon** cut the corner linebacker in two with one of the neatest blocks of the day. Doelling cut back to midfield, got another nifty block from Terpak, glanced over his shoulder and outraced the Green's secondary to score what proved to be the back-breaking touchdown of the game.

Dartmouth's 3rd-string quarterback, Dick Beattie, futilely threw three passes that only seemed to prolong the agony for the defending champs from Hanover, as the ambient Penn line never let up. With no completions on its last series of downs, the visitors' Jack Kinderdine dropped back to kick for his 7th and last time of the day. The clock was running now. One minute, 30 seconds to go. **George Koval** kept for six yards. Koval kept the ball again for six more yards and a 1st down, and finally the ball game was over.

The players upended coach Steve Sebo and carried him to a midfield rendezvous with Dartmouth coach Bob Blackman. The Quaker locker room was a madhouse of backslaps, cheers, and well-dones. Big tackle **Ed Smith** beamed as he spoke: "This is the most wonderful thing that's ever happened around here. We beat Dartmouth. Whew." Reflections of the game brought on yet more cheering thoughts.

The win for the Penn squad was solid, after having lost to its New Hampshire antagonists by a combined 4-point total in the '57 and '58 clashes. Once again we ascended to the top of the towering north stands, finished the work at hand and decided it was time to leave. When we got to a bucket of nuts and bolts we laughingly refer to as a car, we noticed a minor difficulty. One of the back tires was a flat as 3-day-old beer, and the spare was pretzel-soft. But if that is the price of victory, we won't mind if the transmission drops out next week-end.

5. *In the Driver's Seat*

November 7, 1959 - Penn 28, Yale 12

"Jack [Hanlon] gets that 'big man' for me, whoever he is."

Penn Leads Ivy League as Doelling Sets Record

John Seksinsky scores on a 5-yard TD pass from George Koval to give Penn a 19-12 lead.

Led by **Fred Doelling** and **George Koval**, Penn came from behind to overpower Yale with an inspired 28-12 victory, before 25,102 spectators at Homecoming Day 1959. The victory enabled Penn to move into undisputed possession of 1st place in the Ivy League. Taking a 12-0 lead early in the 2nd quarter, Yale appeared well on its way to tag the Quakers with their second loss in a row. However, touchdowns by Doelling and **Dave Coffin** gave Penn a 13-12 half-time lead, which it never relinquished. A recovered fumble led to a Koval-to-**John Seksinsky** aerial score, and, with seconds remaining in the game, Doelling galloped a whopping 71 yards on three successive plays for the final touchdown. By the end of the contest, Doelling had broken **Skip Minisi**'s all-time Penn record for same.

Score by Quarters					
	1	2	3	4	Total
Yale	6	6	0	0	12
Penn	0	13	8	7	28

Scoring Summary
Yale – Blanchard 1 run (kick failed)
Yale – Winkler 1 run (run failed)
Penn – Doelling 10 run (kick failed)
Penn – Coffin 1 run (Shaw kick)
Penn - Seksinsky 5 pass from Koval (Berlinger pass from Koval)
Penn – Doelling 9 run (Shaw kick)
Attendance - 25,102

Doelling Tops Minisi's Mark by William Bates, Sports Editor, Daily Pennsylvanian

When halfback Fred Doelling took a handoff from **Larry Purdy** and streaked around right end for nine yards and Penn's 4th and final score against Yale, the 5-foot-11-inch, 185-pound speedster from Valparaiso, Indiana, wrote a new record into the Penn scoring books that is apt to stay there for some time to come. The hard-nosed Doelling gained his 1,394th yard for the Quakers since gracing the starting 11 as a sophomore. Going into the Eli tilt 139 yards shy of the all-time University record, the battling senior capped a productive 2-touchdown day with a 59-yard jaunt through Yale's tough forward wall – and added insult to injury by carrying the remaining 12 yards into the end zone on two ensuing carries.

But Doelling is quick to shy away from the limelight. He praised his guards who led the plays, he applauded his backfield mate, Dave Coffin, who fills the other halfback spot, and above all he congratulated his fullback, **Jack Hanlon**. "He's the best blocker I've ever had and the best fullback I've ever had the privilege of being with. Jack gets that 'big man' for me, whoever he is." For Doelling, the realization of a new University record was possible only through "a great team effort."

*In this game, **Fred Doelling** became the 1st Penn player to pierce the Yale end-zone on the ground.*

6. Once Upon a Cold Thanksgiving Day

November 26, 1959 - Penn 28, Cornell 13

"Win today, and we walk together forever."

Ivy Champs - Quakers Rally to Win Their 1st Title

*In this now-iconic photograph, Penn Captain **Barney Berlinger** leaps to catch a 4th-quarter touchdown pass from QB **George Koval**. This tied the score at 13-13, and the extra point put Penn ahead to stay. The Quakers went on to win 28-13 and capture their 1st Ivy League title, before 23,661 Thanksgiving Day fans at Franklin Field.*

For nearly 33 minutes, the Red and Blue seemed to be avoiding the Ivy League title. They were tight from tension and appeared to be frozen stiff on this 30-degree Thanksgiving Day. Early in the 3rd quarter, Cornell was leading 13-0, and hopes for the title were dimming. Then, all of a sudden, a chemical change seemed to take place, and on the arm of junior quarterback **George Koval**, the Quakers rose to the challenge.

On 4th down situations, Koval threw 13 yards to **Jack Hanlon** and 25 yards to **Barney Berlinger** for touchdowns. Berlinger's catch was a leaping effort that amazed the entire crowd. Then **Fred Doelling** stole the ball and ran it back into Cornell territory. Koval starred once more, as he threw to **Bill Kesack** for an 8-yard score, and **John Terpak** added the finale on a 1-yard TD plunge. Time ran out, and the Quakers had gained undisputed recognition as champions of the Ivy League for 1959.

Score by Quarters					
	1	2	3	4	Total
Cornell	0	7	6	0	13
Penn	0	0	7	21	28

Scoring Summary
Cornell -   Hoffman 4 pass from McKelvey (Telesh kick)
Cornell -   Sadusky 37 pass from Tino (kick failed)
Penn -   Hanlon 13 pass from Koval (Shaw kick)
Penn -   Berlinger 25 pass from Koval (Shaw kick)
Penn -   Kesack 8 pass from Koval (Shaw kick)
Penn -   Terpak 1 run (Shaw kick)
Attendance – 23,661

Cannon Signals Penn Victory over Cornell, and the Quakers' 1st Ivy League Football Title
   by Alfred Haber, Daily Pennsylvanian

The echoes of the little signal cannon of the Red and Blue cheerleaders boomed from the banks of the Schuylkill to the shores of Lake Cayuga on Thanksgiving Day, as it heralded the crowning of Pennsylvania as Ivy League football champions. Trailing 13-0 behind Cornell's fired-up 11 in the traditional Turkey Day donnybrook on Franklin Field, the determined Quaker attack developed a full head of steam late in the 3rd quarter and carried through its spectacular offensive display in the final one, as the Quaker signal cannon belched after each of the Red and Blue's four touchdown drives.

Jack Hanlon started the Quakers along the victory trail, as he snared a 3rd-period pass from QB George Koval on the Cornell 10-yard line and bulled his way past two defenders into pay-dirt territory. "I was flat on my back after I threw that pass to Hanlon," said Koval. "I didn't know what happened until I heard the cannon go off."

The Quakers were rolling. Seven plays later, **Jim Dunsmore** recovered a Cornell fumble after a wall of Penn tacklers jarred the ball loose from the Big Red's flashy ball-carrier, George Telesh. Within four minutes the little cannon roared again, as Barney Berlinger, the Penn captain, made a spectacular leaping catch of Koval's 25-yard touchdown pass, putting the Quakers ahead to stay. The toy cannon blasted twice more, as an 8-yard bullet-pass from Koval to right-end Bill Kesack and a 2-yard halfback plunge by John Terpak carried into the Cornell end zone, making the score 28-13.

Then it remained only for the Quakers to coast through the few remaining minutes of play, in which the Cornellians drove to within five yards of Red and Blue paydirt but were stopped short of the goal, as time ran out on the season. The concluding boom, which signaled the Penn victory, probably also reverberated through a special radio hook-up relaying the contest back to an eager audience in Hanover, New Hampshire, shattering Dartmouth's hopes for a 2nd straight Ivy League championship.

1959: That Championship Season
The euphoria of winning the Ivy League championship did not last long. The following Monday, the University of Pennsylvania announced that it had fired head coach Steve Sebo. The university had made the decision earlier, so winning the title came too late to save the coach. The players objected, but to no avail. For better or worse (it turned out to be the latter), the **John Stiegman** era was about to begin.

1959 Ivy League Champions

*Penn passing wizard **George Koval** (10).*

Penn Head Coach Steve Sebo celebrates the Quakers' 1st Ivy League title with his players.

Recollection from Barney Berlinger, Class of 1960

For me, the most memorable segment of the '59 Team's run to the Ivy Championship was the last 17 minutes of the Cornell game at Franklin Field. We were down 13-0, with only 17 minutes left. If we won, we would claim the outright Ivy Championship. If we lost, Dartmouth, whom we beat 13-0 in our opener, would be the champion.

Jack Hanlon made a great play and scored with less than the 17 minutes left. Then, still late in the 3rd quarter, it was 4th down and short yardage in Cornell territory. Hanlon made another great grab for a 1st down to keep our attack going (if it had gone incomplete, we would have lost possession, and time was becoming a factor).

Now it was again 4th down, on the Cornell 25. George Koval fired a long pass to me, and (thank God) I caught it. So Penn now lead 14-13. Shortly thereafter George fired another TD to Billy Kesack. 21-13 Penn. The Big Red tried a 4th-down desperation play which failed, and Penn took over deep in Cornell territory. Johnny Terpak fires over the goal line for a 4th score in less than 17 minutes, and we took the Ivy crown outright. 28-13 Penn. What a great team! I love every one of them to this day.

7. *Who Loves Harvard?*

November 2, 1963 – Penn 7, Harvard 2

"Ten thousand men of Harvard want vict'ry today."

Quakers Concede Safety to Shock Crimson

A rare happy moment for coach John Stiegman and his team, after the Quakers upset Harvard.

Rarely is a safety against your own team the most exciting play of the game. Rarer still is when that safety is the key play that leads to victory by your team. But that is precisely what happened in this game, in which Harvard, possessor of a 9-game undefeated streak and co-leaders of the Ivy League, fell at Franklin Field before an inspired Penn team, in Eastern football's greatest upset of the 1963 season.

Penn combined the running of **Bruce Molloy** and **Whit Smith** with its finest defensive effort in four years, to completely dominate the game until late in the 4th quarter. Divine intervention, in the form of the *"Sports Illustrated* jinx" may have contributed to the upset also: Two days after appearing on the magazine's cover, the Crimson carried the nation's longest winning streak to Philadelphia, along with title hopes. But Penn coach John Stiegman and his team were waiting for them.

Defeating Harvard for the 1st time in his coaching career, Stiegman abandoned his "open" style of play for ultra-conservative football – until late in the 4th quarter. Stay tuned. Basing his strategy on the excellent punting of Molloy and downfield punt recoveries, Stiegman forced Harvard to play much of the game inside its own 10-yard line. After two periods, the score was still 0-0, and Harvard began to appear unnerved. Penn won the coin toss before the 2nd half opened – as was the practice then – and elected to kick off to the Crimson, hoping to force them into a mistake. That mistake came when Harvard fumbled the kick. The blunder set up the only touchdown of the game.

After Penn recovered the fumble, Molloy and Smith together carried the ball a combined eight times for 24 yards and a touchdown. An 8-yard sprint by Smith gave Penn a 1st down on the 2-yard line, and, two plays later, Molloy plunged in for the touchdown, putting the Quakers ahead 7-0. With Molloy's punts continually pinning the Crimson deep in their own territory, the score remained the same late into the 4th quarter. After Penn once again stopped a Harvard threat, it found itself backed up to its own end zone, with a 4th down and with under five minutes to play.

Stiegman now took the boldest step in his tenure as Penn coach: He ordered Molloy to drop back in the end zone and run back and forth until being tackled by the Crimson for a safety, instead of punting. The reasoning was basic: Molloy was kicking into a strong wind, and Stiegman did not want to chance a short punt and a long runback. Molloy did as instructed, making the score 7-2.

Penn kicked off from the 20, and Harvard returned the ball to the Penn 45-yard line with just over three minutes to play. Until now, the punting of Molloy and great pass coverage by the Penn defense had kept the Crimson deep in its own territory. Now in Penn territory, Harvard opened up an intense aerial game. On 1st and 10 from the Penn 20, a Harvard pass glanced off the intended receiver's fingertips. Two more plays failed, and on the 4th down, the entire Penn secondary combined to knock down a pass.

Harvard managed to snag the ball for one more play, but **Fred Levin** intercepted a last-second, desperation pass. The entire Penn team raced out to the center of the field, with Coach Stiegman on its shoulders, and the 11,144 fans roared their approval of the Quakers' biggest victory in four years. "Who loves Harvard? We do!"

Score by Quarters					
	1	2	3	4	Total
Harvard	0	0	0	2	2
Penn	0	7	0	0	7

Scoring Summary
Penn -   Molloy 2 run (Henderson kick)
Harvard -   Safety, Molloy tackled in end zone
Attendance – 11,144

The "Kiss of Death" by Dan Rottenberg, Sports Editor, *Daily Pennsylvanian*
We saw Penn's victory in the cards as early as Thursday night. That afternoon we had taken considerable ribbing from our fellow staff men for picking Harvard to beat Penn in the D.P. Grid Picks. We felt a bit sheepish about it ourselves, but after predicting Penn victories five weeks in a row, one could hardly maintain impartial standing by going against as heavy a favorite as Harvard.

Several hours later we returned to our humble abode and, before getting down to work, leafed through the newest issue of *Sports Illustrated*. We were casually glancing through it, you understand, when suddenly we sat bolt upright in our seat. Historical Inevitability. There, staring us in the face, was a piece titled "Who Loves Harvard?," praising the Crimson to the skies, complete with action photos and a close-up of a comely Radcliffe bosom adorned by a "Fight Fiercely Harvard" pin.

Familiar as we are with *Sports Illustrated*'s influence on athletic events, we realized there was just one thing to be done. We raced to the phone and called the printer. "Stop the presses," we screamed frantically. "Change Rottenberg's prediction that Penn can't lose on Saturday." Unfortunately, the *Daily Pennsylvanian* finished printing early, and our "Harvard 14, Penn 3" prognostication had to stand.

But that was a small price to pay for a deliriously happy weekend. Have you ever seen condemned men play football? Harvard gave us some idea of what it must be like that Saturday. Right from the opening kickoff the Harvards, 9-game streak and all, seemed to realize that they didn't have a chance. Mere mortals can't erase the *Sports Illustrated* kiss of death. Even *Sports Illustrated*, though, never planted quite as powerful a kiss as this one.

What hit Penn that weekend? Kiss of death? Fate? Mother Nature? Determination? Skill? We're not asking any questions. Suffice it to say that we loved every minute of it. From where we stood, several things happened at 3:37: a fellow named **Fred Levin** clung to a football; a roar erupted from Franklin Field's South Stands; jubilant players in red and blue carried a crew-cutted man in a suit across the field; dejected men in crimson and white dragged off to their lockers, shocked beyond comprehension of what had happened; the clock showed no time remaining; and most important of all, the scoreboard read "Pennsylvania 7, Harvard 2."

1963: A Lone Bright Spot
The upset of Harvard was the lone highlight of John Stiegman's 5-year tenure. The Quakers won no more games the rest of that season and won only one game (a non-league contest against Lehigh) the following year. After a 5-year overall record of 12-33, Penn showed Stiegman the door at the end of the 1964 season. He was replaced by **Bob Odell**, a former Penn All-American.

Recollection from John Doman, Class of 1966
That was my sophomore year, I was playing in the defensive backfield, and that game was the highlight of my three varsity seasons. It was a

beautiful fall day in Philadelphia, and Harvard was coming into Franklin Field with an undefeated record, nine straight wins, and a cover story in *Sports Illustrated* the previous week. We were big-time underdogs.

As it happened, the Harvard quarterback, Billy Humenuk, was a Philly guy (Lincoln High), and the local papers were writing about his coming home. As a Philly guy myself (North Catholic), I was particularly psyched for this game. It turned out to be a defensive battle, and we had them shut out 7-0 in the final minutes of the game. We had the ball within our own 10-yard line and couldn't get it out of there. On 4th down, Bruce Molloy, our star running back and punter, went back to (assumingly) punt it out of the end zone. However, Coach Stiegman had called for Molloy to run time off the clock by running back and forth in the end zone as long as he could until taken down, giving Harvard two points but giving us a more advantageous position to kick the ball. They got the ball, and we were able to shut them down in the final two minutes, ending their undefeated streak.

Some say it was the *Sports Illustrated* curse. I prefer to think our defensive team rose to the occasion. This game that certainly deserves to be on this list.

Recollection from Fred Levin, Class of 1964

If my memory is correct, I did not play a big role in this game. I had an injury, so I decided to play it safe and hang back in my safety position, not rushing forward to tackle anybody and risk letting anyone get behind me. I might have intercepted a pass toward the end of the game when the Harvard quarterback was throwing Hail-Mary passes in a desperate attempt to even the score. I thought I got away with my conservative playing, but I remember the next day one of the coaches commenting that I looked like a turkey out there. So I guess I didn't fool a knowledgeable observer.

It was certainly a remarkable game for the team. Harvard had one of the best teams in the Ivy League that year, and we had one of the worst. We came into the game big underdogs. Why we won is a puzzle. But the strategy Stiegman adopted – winning the toss but electing to kick off – was certainly unusual and seemed to pay off. Also, deliberately causing a safety at the end of the game, so that we could maintain our lead and get to kick off again, was genius on his part. I guess it reflected his view that our defense was a lot better than our offense.

Note from the author: It appears that Mr. Levin is too modest. More than one observer said that Levin was the best player on the field that day, and his interception at the end certainly played a huge role in the outcome.

8. We Got Our Kicks

October 30, 1965 – Penn 10, Harvard 10

"It was worse than it should have been, but better than it might have been."

Lynch's "Un-intentional" Kick Leaves Harvard Fit to Be Tied

Penn's Tom Owen (25) blocks Maurey Dullea's 2nd period field goal attempt. Penn's Dennis Lynch finally fell on the ball way downfield, setting up the Quakers' 2nd score of the day.

In a game in which the final score was determined mathematically by intentional kicks, a possibly unintentional kick was probably the key play. (Will explain later).

Harvard and Penn played 60 minutes of hard-nosed football without reaching a verdict, as 16,413 Homecoming fans saw the exciting 10-10 tie. With the accent on "defense-when-it-counted," Penn played the role of opportunist, capitalizing on two breaks to score a 1st-period touchdown and a 2nd-period field goal. Harvard, just as its head coach John Yovicsin had feared, failed to attain any offensive consistency. Even with a number of good scoring opportunities, the Crimson failed to come up with a "big" play when it counted most. On the other hand, the Quakers scored the 2nd time they had the ball.

After defensive tackle **John Rodgers** recovered a Harvard bobble on the 9-yard line, **Pete Wisniewski** moved the squad down to the Crimson 3. There, in an obvious 4th-down field goal situation, Odell faked the kick and had his quarterback fire a touchdown strike to **Bill McGill** in the end zone. With 6:08 gone in the 1st period, the Quakers led 7-0. But after the ensuing kickoff and an exchange of punts, the Crimson marched 53 yards in nine plays to even the ledger at 7-7.

Early in the 2nd period, Quaker **Tom Owen** broke through to block a Harvard field-goal attempt. The ball bounded crazily, and then Penn defensive end **Dennis Lynch** kicked it far down the field, eventually falling on the ball. After a looong discussion, the referees agreed that Lynch's kick had been *un*-intentional, so the Quakers took over on Harvard's 33-yard stripe. Six plays later, **Carl Henderson** entered the game to try a field goal. This time there was no fake, as the sophomore specialist toed a perfect 31 yarder to give Penn a half-time bulge of 10-7.

After a scoreless 3rd quarter, the visitors evened the score the 1st time they had the ball in the 4th. McGill, punting from his own end zone, was forced to hurry his kick, and Harvard took over on the Penn 39. After a 1st down, the Crimson attack stalled, and their kicker Maurey Dullea was called on to make his 3rd field goal attempt of the day. From the 28, Dullea lofted the ball just high enough so that when it hit the cross bar, instead of a "doink," the ball bounced up and over for the three points, evening the score at 10-10.

Harvard threatened again at the end of the game, but a last-second desperation field goal attempt by Jim Babcock from the 35 was short and to the right, giving the underdog Quakers a tie, and leaving the homecoming crowd with the feeling that "it was worse than it should have been, but better than it might have been." Considering that

Harvard was the clear favorite in this game, this was a moral victory for the Red and Blue

.

Score by Quarters					
	1	2	3	4	Total
Harvard	7	0	0	3	**10**
Penn	7	3	0	0	**10**

Scoring Summary
Penn -   McGill 3 pass from Wisniewski (Henderson kick)
Harvard -   Choquette 3 run (Dullea kick)
Penn -   Henderson 31 FG
Harvard -   Dullea 28 FG
Attendance – 16,413

9. Lion Taming

November 13, 1965 – Penn 31, Columbia 21

"When they got us angry, we knew we would win."

Penn Rallies from 21-0 Deficit to Beat Columbia

Penn wingback **Rick Owens** *heads for the end zone with a* **Bill Creeden** *pass in the 4th quarter. Owens scored twice, had eight receptions, bringing his total for the year to 31, a Penn record.*

During this Penn victory, only one team appeared to be on the field at a time. For the 1st 20 minutes, it was all Columbia, as the Lions set up a 21-0 margin over a non-existent Penn defense. And for the last 40 minutes, the Red and Blue forced the Lions to eat dirt for the 1st time in six years, as quarterback **Bill Creeden** moved the Quakers for 31 straight points. The Quaker victory guaranteed, also for the 1st time in six years, at least a .500 season for the Red and Blue.

Columbia picked the Penn defense apart during the 1st quarter and part of the 2nd. The Lions jumped out to a 21-0 lead, causing their coach Buff Donelli to jump with glee on the sidelines, thinking that Penn could never pull itself out of such a hole. However, as head coach Bob Odell said after the game, "Enthusiasm is our key point. We just didn't have it during the 1st period, but when they got us angry, we knew we would win." Ahead 21-0, Columbia drove to the Quaker 1-yard line early in the 2nd period. But the Red and Blue held, and from then on it was all Penn.

The Quakers *were* angry. **Rick Owens** returned a Lion punt 47 yards, **Jody Allen** got into a fight, and Odell ran on the field. Allen was ejected, but now the Quakers' blood was up. Creeden passes to Owens and **Bill McGill** accounted for Penn's 1st touchdown, at 14:31 in the 2nd quarter. Then **Jock Hannum** performed a successful on-sides kick, and Penn had the ball on the Lions' 42. Two more Creeden-to-Owens passes and then one to **Bill Workman** put Penn on the Columbia 9. A 25-yard field goal attempt by **Carl Henderson** was good, and the half ended with the score 21-10; Penn had scored twice in 28 seconds. "I couldn't hold them in the locker room," said Odell. "They just wanted to get back at Columbia." In the 2nd half, the Penn defense proceeded to maul the Lions, with Columbia gaining less than 10 yards in the 3rd period.

Meanwhile Creeden passed to Owens for the 2nd Penn touchdown, to Workman for the 3rd, and then finally to Owens again, to put the icing on the cake at 31-21. The sophomore quarterback set a Penn record: 14 completions in an Ivy league game. Owens set two Penn records: eight catches in an Ivy game and 31 pass receptions in a season. The team carried coach Odell off the field in celebration. They weren't angry anymore, as one of the greatest comebacks in Penn history had just taken place.

Franklin Field Saturdays

Score by Quarters					
	1	2	3	4	Total
Columbia	14	7	0	0	21
Penn	0	10	7	14	31

Scoring Summary
Columbia – Ballantine 5 run (Burns kick)
Columbia – Tosi 8 run (Burns kick)
Columbia – Dennis 56 fumble recovery (Burns kick)
Penn – McGill 1 run (Henderson kick)
Penn – Henderson 25 FG
Penn – Owens 10 pass from Creeden (Henderson kick)
Penn – Workman 24 pass from Creeden (Henderson kick)
Penn – Owens 2 pass from Creeden (Henderson kick)
Attendance – 9,382

1965: New Coach = New Hope
The hiring of head coach Bob Odell, a former Penn All-American running back, thrilled Quaker fans. And indeed, in his 1st season, the team played with a new, fiery spirit and came close to upsetting league leaders Dartmouth and Yale. However, Penn's chance for a winning record for the 1st time in six years was thwarted by – you guessed it – an uninspiring 38-14 Thanksgiving Day loss to Cornell at Franklin Field. The next two seasons proved disappointing, as the Quakers managed only a 5-13 record overall.

10. Tiger Taming

October 26, 1968 -

"Hold that Tiger!"

Penn beats Princeton, Remains Unbeaten

Jerry Santini *(30) goes up and over to give Penn its 1st score in the Red and Blue's victory over Princeton. 30,886 spectators watched the Homecoming spectacle.*

"I had to get back at them, and I was in the right place at the right time."
George Burrell, Penn defensive back

This year was different. This year, it finally happened. Princeton made the mistakes, and the Quakers capitalized. The result was a sweet 19-14 victory, putting Penn's record at a perfect 5-0, the 1st unbeaten 5-game streak since 1948 and the 1st Princeton defeat in nine years.

The sweetness belonged to coach Bob Odell and a long list of individual stars. The defense showed its prowess by holding the much-feared Tiger running game scoreless for three quarters, while their own offensive teammates scrambled to a 19-0 lead, battling the wind and a stubborn Princeton defense. Quarterback **Bernie Zbrzeznj** continued to prove his ability in the clutch by effectively guiding the offense to a 1st-period score, capitalizing on defensive tackle **Jim Fuddy**'s interception. The sophomore lineman's catch was on a deflected pass by **Chuck Aho**, giving the Quakers the ball on the Princeton 23-yard line. After a 20-yard screen pass from Zbrzeznj to fullback **Bill Sudhaus**, senior **Jerry Santini** tumbled over from the 1. The **Eliot Berry** point-after gave Penn a 7-0 lead.

The half ended with Penn on top 10-0, and Berry's 2nd field goal and a 3rd-quarter 18-yard TD pass from Zbrzeznj to tight-end **Dave Graham** put the Quakers in what appeared to be a commanding 19-0 lead. However, Princeton blocked the point-after attempt, and things began to change. When the teams switched sides at the end of the quarter, the most noticeable change was the wind. The 18-mph breeze had been with the Quakers for the entire 1st and 3rd quarters. With the wind now at their back, Princeton wasted no time, completing a 57-yard touchdown bomb on the 2nd play.

As if a dark cloud were suddenly settling over, Zbrzeznj and Santini were unable to get the club moving and establish the all-important, time-consuming ground game. The Princeton offense seemed to come alive, and Princeton moved quickly for another score - an 11-yard run for a touchdown. With over nine minutes left in the game and Penn now ahead by only 19-14, the contest became extremely tense.

Penn picked up one 1st down but had to turn over the ball. The ensuing punt put Princeton on their own 27 with six minutes to go. With the Quakers' backs to the ropes and their defense tiring, Princeton tried the deep pattern that brought their 1st score. This time, defensive back **George Burrell** intercepted at the Penn 37. "I had to get back at them," said Burrell, "and I was in the right place at the right time." Two long minutes remained against a tough Tiger defense, and the seconds ticked away sluggishly for the Penn rooters. Again, still facing a stiff wind and a fierce Tiger defense, the Quakers had to cede possession with just over a minute remaining. Burrell's time came again, and the senior safety laid back and picked off his 2nd Princeton pass. His 6-yard return enabled Zbrzeznj to sit on the ball, and the happy Quakers left the field with their 1st winning season since 1959, and their 1st victory over Princeton since that year.

The Quakers were now on top of the Ivy League, in a tie with their next two opponents, Harvard and Yale.

***George Burrell** (42) saves the win over Princeton with his 2nd interception of the day.*

Franklin Field Saturdays

Score by Quarters					
	1	2	3	4	Total
Princeton	0	0	0	14	14
Penn	7	3	9	0	19

Scoring Summary
Penn –   Santini 1 rush (Berry kick)
Penn –   Berry 25 FG
Penn –   Berry 39 FG
Penn–   Graham 18 pass from Zbrzeznj (kick blocked)
Princeton –   Coleman 57 pass from McCullough (Holtberg kick)
Princeton –   McCullough 11 run (Holtberg kick)
Attendance – 30,886

11. Scout's Honor

November 23, 1968 – Penn 26, Dartmouth 21

"I thought I was never going to play on a winning team again."

50,188 See Quakers Beat Big Green

*Penn QB **Bernie Zbrzeznj** (12) uncorks one of his 24 pass attempts against Dartmouth while getting blocking help from **Jerry Santini** (30) and **Tom Hamlin** (75).*

After many pre-season "experts" deemed Penn to be the worst team in the East, the Quakers wrapped up their finest football season in nine years with a thrilling 26-21 victory over favored Dartmouth. It was Penn's 3rd upset win in an amazing year, in which they finished with a 7-2 record. This was their 1st winning record since 1959, and this victory over Dartmouth landed them in 3rd-place in the Ivy League, behind Harvard and Yale. I thought I was never going to play on a winning team again," said Penn linebacker **Frank Pfeilmeier**.

Franklin Field Saturdays

A huge swarm of 50,188 fans, including 24,000 Boy Scouts – the largest crowd at a Penn home football game since the 1954 clash with Notre Dame – filled Franklin Field to see if the Quakers could shock Dartmouth in the same fashion in which they had upset Cornell and Princeton earlier in the year. Despite the Scouts' cheers of "We want Penn," Dartmouth gained an early 7-0 lead, driving 73 yards in 10 plays for the score.

But Penn then embarked on one of its finest offensive productions of the season, gaining 416 yards against the Dartmouth defense. Quarterback **Bernie Zbrzeznj** got the Quaker offense rolling by hitting **Pete Blumenthal** on two consecutive down-and-out patterns. A few plays later, with the ball on the Dartmouth 13, Blumenthal faked the down-and-out pattern and then broke to the end zone to take a perfect pass from Zbrzeznj, tying the score at 7-7. Early in the 2nd quarter, throwing from deep in his own territory, Zbrzeznj hurled the only interception of the day, and Dartmouth returned it to the Penn 4-yard line. Penn's defense made a gallant goal line stand, but on 4th down, the Big Green managed to bull it over from the 1, making the score 14-7. Penn tied it again, with 50 seconds left before the half ended, as Zbrzeznj engineered an 81-yard drive in 11 plays, with halfback **Jerry Santini** spinning into the end zone for the touchdown for the final two yards.

Early in the 3rd quarter, after a Penn drive stalled at the Dartmouth 6-yard line, **Eliot Berry** kicked his 11th field goal of the season, putting Penn on top by 17-14. With 3:30 left in the 3rd quarter, Santini burst through the Dartmouth line for 13 yards, becoming the Quakers' all-time career rushing leader with 1,593 yards. Simultaneously he set the team's season record with 880 yards, breaking the mark of 830 yards set by **Cabot Knowlton** a year earlier, (done with the assistance of a blocking back named Santini).

Ken Dunn capped the drive by scoring Penn's final 1968 touchdown on a 9-yard sprint around left end, with 34 seconds to play in the 3rd quarter. Berry's conversion made it 24-14 entering the final stanza. **Bill Sudhaus** legged a booming punt, leading to the Dartmouth punt returner being carried back by Penn defenders into the end zone for a safety. Penn now led 26-14. Dartmouth managed to close the gap to 26-21, but Penn's defense proved too tough in the end. **John Brown** halted a late Big Green drive with a brilliant interception in the end zone, and the entire Penn secondary spelled the end of the last Dartmouth thrust by completely blanketing the Dartmouth receivers. The victory was finally Penn's - its 1st over Dartmouth since 1959. The players carried coach Odell off the field, and the Boy Scouts cheered their approval of a winning football team.

Score by Quarters	1	2	3	4	Total
Dartmouth	7	7	0	7	21
Penn	7	7	10	2	26

Scoring Summary
Dartmouth – Beier 2 run (P. Donovan kick)
Penn – Blumenthal 13 pass from Zbrzeznj (Berry kick)
Dartmouth – Chartrand 1 run (P. Donovan kick)
Penn – Santini 2 run (Berry kick)
Penn – Berry 23 FG
Penn – Dunn 9 run (Berry kick)
Penn – Safety, Quinn tackled in end zone
Dartmouth – Beier 3 run (P. Donovan kick)
Attendance – 50,188

1968: Best of the Rest
After the great victory over Princeton, the Quakers had to play consecutive games against the two teams who turned out to be the best in the league – Harvard and Yale. Not totally unexpectedly, the Red and Blue were soundly defeated in both. However, the exciting victory in the finale against Dartmouth gave Penn its best record in nine years, and with their so-called Class of Destiny (1970) returning, there was genuine optimism that the Quakers were going to contend for the title in 1969.

12. This Guy's the 3rd Stringer?

October 4, 1969 – Penn 23, Brown 2

"Put Me in, Coach, I'm Ready to Play"

Procacci 'Phils' In for Zbrzeznj – Penn Wins

Phil Procacci *fires a pass against Brown, after taking over at QB for* ***Bernie Zbrzeznj.***

> "Me."
> **Bob Odell** (Penn head coach), when asked by a reporter whom he would he would have put in at quarterback if Phil Procacci had gotten injured.

An ill wind chilled the spines of thousands of Red-and-Blue rooters, when, late in the 1st quarter, the Franklin Field public address system delivered an ominous announcement: "Penn quarterback **Bernie Zbrzeznj** has suffered a total shoulder separation." On the field, the Quakers seemed locked in the grip of defeat. The season, with its title aspirations, was vanishing quickly, and the stage was set for an upset. Only it never happened. The Quaker team pulled together behind 3rd-string sophomore quarterback **Phil Procacci** and a truly inspired defense, to batter the Bruins, 23-2.

Despite losing Zbrzeznj, Penn didn't die - the day belonged to Procacci, despite a shaky start. The Hollywood, Florida native replaced QB **Mike Hickok** (Zbrzeznj's replacement), *who had suffered the same fate* on the 1st play of the 2nd quarter. Procacci stepped in, throwing TD tosses of 60 and 25 yards to ends **Dave Graham** and **Pete Blumenthal**. And he ran 69 yards himself for Penn's other touchdown. On his 1st play, Procacci was gang-tackled in the end zone for a safety, which gave the Bruins a short-lived 2-0 lead. The visitors, however, could not shake their jinx at Franklin Field, where they had not won since 1911. No fewer than six interceptions by Penn defenders kept the Bruins from mounting a TD drive.

Head coach Bob Odell, emotionally spent, revealed at a post-game press conference that Procacci had not practiced at the quarterback slot in a month. "We had been using him at cornerback but shifted him to offensive halfback last week when **Bill Sudhaus** was hurt. One thing for sure, we knew he was a heck of an athlete. He always seems to come up with a big play." The 1st big play was the TD bomb to Graham, which electrified the 21,603 fans. On that 3rd-down play, Procacci ran to his left after faking a handoff. The entire Brown line met the fullback, with Penn needing only a yard for the 1st down. Graham, meanwhile, looking like he was going to block somebody, slipped a few yards in back of the Brown defenders. Procacci put the ball right in Graham's hands, and the senior end outran two Bruins to the end zone.

Eliot Berry added a 34-yard field goal before the half ended. Then Procacci kept the Quakers moving in explosive fashion throughout the 3rd and 4th quarters. On his 69-yard TD gallop, he faked to the fullback, sending the Brown flow in one direction and then cut back in the other. "I thought, hey, maybe we'll get a 1st down," said Odell. "Then I saw Phil outrunning them all. I didn't realize he was that fast."

Procacci's speed was also instrumental in his TD toss to split-end Blumenthal. Aided by a vicious block from fullback **Bob Long**, Procacci fled to his right and fired a bullet cross-field to Blumenthal, who took the ball over his left shoulder while running full tilt into the end zone. "The team pulled together," said Procacci after the game. "The defense was outstanding. My 1st play was a little shaky, but I became more confident as the game progressed, and I had a hell of a team behind me."

He certainly did: the Bruins opened up as if they were going to blow out the Quakers early. Their offensive thrusts, however, stayed confined between the '20's;' when they got close, the Red and Blue dug in and refused to budge. **Jim Fuddy** came up with 13 unassisted tackles and was in on innumerable others. **Mike Chwastyk** and **Dave Pottruck** made nine tackles apiece, while defensive back **Steve Kenoyer** made seven. And then there were the six interceptions.

As Bob Odell wrapped up his press conference, a newsman asked, "Who would you have put in if Procacci had gotten hurt?" Odell hesitated for a split second, smiled, and replied, "Me."

Score by Quarters					
	1	2	3	4	Total
Brown	2	0	0	0	2
Penn	0	10	7	6	23

Scoring Summary
Brown -   Safety, Procacci tackled in end zone
Penn -   Graham 60, pass from Procacci (Berry kick)
Penn -   Berry 34 FG
Penn -   Procacci 69, run (Berry kick)
Penn -   Blumenthal 25, pass from Procacci (kick failed)
Attendance - 21,603

1969: Buzzard's Luck
This was to have been *The Year*, but the injury to star QB Bernie Zbrzeznj was too devastating a blow to overcome. Phil Procacci's performance in the Brown game offered some hope, but Procacci himself suffered a season-ending injury two games later, leaving 4th-stringer **Terry Groome** to mop up against Lehigh. The Quakers were 3-1 at that point, but that was as good as it got. The coaches ultimately switched **John Brown** - a defensive back - to quarterback, and he performed more than admirably, but it was too little, too late – the Quakers would defeat only Columbia the rest of the way. Despite the injuries, Penn still had a chance for a winning season, but it was – wait for it – stopped by a 28-14 loss to Cornell, in the season finale at Franklin Field.

13. *So Close*

October 24, 1970 - Princeton 22, Penn 16

"Hang Jeff Davis on a sour apple tree."

Quakers Almost Win After Final Gun Sounds

Penn quarterback **Pancho Micir** *(9) gets set to loft a pass. Although hobbled by a sprained ankle, Micir played brilliantly.*

"It would have been a great one to win."
Bob Odell, Penn Head Coach

The game is never over until the clock runs out. Sometimes it's not even over then. Princeton beat Penn 22-16, but only by holding up against three Quaker threats in the last two minutes, including a do-or-die play from the Tiger 5-yard line *after* the final gun. The visitors came up with two interceptions and a game-saving deflection to pull out the win, and the 36,478 fans were treated to the most exciting conclusion to an Ivy League game since the 1968 Harvard-Yale classic – so exciting, in fact, that fans on both sides of the stadium gave a standing ovation to both teams at the end. When Princeton quarterback Rod Plummer handed off to Hank Bjorklund for what figured to be the game's last play, a funny thing happened: Bjorklund lost the ball as he was hit, and Penn defensive end **Dick Cowan** fell on it at the Quaker 49, with eight seconds left in the game. But back to that later...

The 1st half was a defensive struggle, ending in the odd score of Penn 3, Princeton 2. On the 1st play of the 2nd quarter, the Quakers' **Bill Heffernan** recovered his teammate Phil Procacci's fumble, but Heffernan's knee touched the ground in the end zone as he did, and the referee ruled a safety. On the last play of the same quarter, **Eliot Berry** - the most prolific kicker in Penn history - pop-flied a 37-yarder that just made it over the uprights. Princeton finally got across the goal line in the 3rd quarter, scoring on a Bjorklund 5-yard sweep, and on a quarterback sneak, giving the Tigers a 15-3 advantage after three periods.

On the 1st play of the final quarter however, Penn QB **Pancho Micir** capped a 78-yard drive by hitting fullback **Bob Long** for a 5-yard TD. Berry's kick was wide to the left - the 1st time he missed in 1970 - and the Quakers trailed 15-9. The next series produced what would prove to be the winning points, with the Tigers driving 80 yards for a touchdown, and using up almost 10 minutes in the process. Micir then took the Quakers 76 yards, culminating in a **Bob Hoffman** touchdown, and setting the stage for a wild final two minutes:

After Hoffman ran six yards for the touchdown and Berry kicked the point with 2:03 left, Penn trailed the bigger and deeper Princeton team by what turned out to be the final score. No one, including the receiving team, was surprised when Berry dribbled the ensuing kickoff down the left side of the field in an attempt at an onside kick and recovery. The result was more startling, however: The ball dribbled through six Tigers, and Penn safety **Steve Kenoyer** fell on it at the Princeton 42.

There should have been 1:50 left in the game, but the clock operator neglected to note the change of possession, and kept the time running as the Quaker offense rushed onto the field. The mistake cost the Quakers 25 or 30 seconds. Micir, who played brilliantly, threw over the middle for **Paul Visokey**, but Princeton picked off the pass. *Strike one* on the Quakers.

Princeton tried to kill the remaining time by giving the ball to workhorse halfback Bjorklund, but a determined Penn defense held him to a net loss of a yard in three tries, forcing a punt. With the Quakers calling timeout after each play, 1:08 still remained. Starting at the Penn 41, Micir threw up the middle to Hoffman, but it popped off Hoffman's hands and into those of Tiger defensive back Barry Richardson at the Princeton 40. With 59 ticks left on the clock and the Red and Blue out of timeouts, the Tigers had the ball and what looked like a lock on the win. *Strike 2*.

And then Bjorklund fumbled, and Penn recovered at its own 49. With 0:08 left, the Tigers put seven men deep, so Micir went in front of them, hitting **Bruce Batch** for 22 yards to the Penn 29, now with only 0:02 to go. Taking the snap from on the referee's ball-in-play signal, Micir looked for Batch over the middle, but the receiver got nowhere near the ball, as he had been interfered with as he cut for daylight. Princeton picked off the pass, and the game appeared over. However, after what seemed like an eternity, a reluctant back judge threw a flag for pass interference. One more shot for the Quakers, from the 5-yard line. Micir tried a hook pass to **Pete "Lucky" Luciano**, who had used his 6'5" frame to make two fine leaping catches earlier. "I just tried to drill the ball in there," said Micir, "but it wasn't drilled hard enough." Ironically-named Princeton free safety Jeff Davis got just enough of his fingertips on the ball to deflect it away, finally giving the Tigers the win, and hanging a sour-apple loss on a gutsy, never-say-die Penn team. *Strike 3*.

Score by Quarters					
	1	2	3	4	Total
Princeton	0	2	13	7	**22**
Penn	0	3	0	13	**16**

Scoring Summary
Princeton –   Safety – Penn recovered fumble in own end zone
Penn –   Berry 37 FG
Princeton –   Bjorklund 5 run (Bartges kick)
Princeton –   Plummer 1 run (pass failed)
Penn –   Long 5 pass from Micir (kick failed)
Princeton –   Williams 3 run (Bartges kick)
Penn –   Hoffman 6 run (Berry kick)
Attendance – 36,478

1970: Another One Bites the Dust
The close loss to Princeton was followed by two not-so-close losses to Harvard and Yale, and ultimately, another losing (4-5) season. With one year still left on his contract, Bob Odell chose to resign. Odell was replaced by **Harry Gamble**, a successful head coach at Lafayette.

14. *Son of So Close*

October 30, 1971 - Harvard 28, Penn 27

"They laughed at us, but they're not laughing now. They know they were damn lucky to win."

Clune's Catches Can't Catch Crimson

Penn split end **Don Clune** *attempts a getaway after catching a 58-yard bomb from* **Gary Shue**. *The talented receiver stole all of the praise in this game, breaking one Ivy record and tying another.*

The scene was the Penn-Harvard Halloween party on a Saturday afternoon in 1971 at Franklin Field, won by the Crimson 28-27 before 21,770 homecoming fans. The Crimson failed to hand over a treat to the Quakers and held a 28-21 lead with time running out in the contest. The home team came up with a trick so well planned, it turned the Harvard secondary into statues, who stood around watching Penn split-end **Don Clune** haul in a 76-yard touchdown bomb.

Third-string quarterback **Mark Mandel** had suddenly appeared on the field in a 3rd and 17 situation on the Penn 24, and, after taking a lateral pass from QB **Gary Shue**, unleashed a touchdown pass to Clune that went 55 yards in the air. Now it was 28-27, and the Quakers lined up to go for two more points and the win. With the Red and Blue flooding the right side of the end zone, **Mike Brumbach** was open, but the pass from Shue was behind him. The ball bounced off Brumbach's hands and hit the AstroTurf out of his diving reach. Harvard fans could breathe again. The next time the Red and Blue got the football. Harvard intercepted on the 2nd down, and that was the ballgame.

"Remember, we lost three ball games on passes dropped like that in the 4th period," said a relieved Crimson coach, Joe Restic, after the game. "We should be 6-0." If the Quakers had executed the passing attack they showed in this game all year long, they might have been 6-0, too. Shue connected for 276 yards and three TDs. Two of the paydirt strikes were to Clune on the game's 1st two series of downs, for 73 and 32 yards respectively. Clune, who was slipping away from everybody all day long, hauled in eight receptions for 284 yards to break the old yardage record of 214 set by Columbia's Bill Wazevich in 1967. His three TD catches allowed his name to be added in the record books, also. "They were playing me to the outside," said the 6'4" soph phenom. "I ran straight at them, and they kept backing up, so I ran right past them."

"He has deceptive speed," Harvard roverback Dave Ignacio said about Clune, "He runs real easy and then bursts by you." The 14-0 Quaker margin, however, failed to unnerve the Crimson, as the visitors erupted for three scores before the half ended, to take the lead, 21-14. Harvard scored from one yard out on a sneak to cap a 88-yard march in the 3rd period, before Shue clicked with fullback **Glenn Gaetano** on an 11-yard scoring toss on the next series of downs, to make it 28-21. The Quakers appeared to be on their way to tie the score early in the 4th period, when **Steve Solow** returned a punt 40 yards through all 11 Harvard players to reach that team's 34. But the Red and Blue had to turn over the ball on the 14, when the ref got out his micrometer to show they were short of a 1st down. The Quakers got the ball back once again, leading to the last Clune touchdown of the day and the failed 2-

point conversion try near the end of the game. "I think we showed a lot of things today," said Shue afterward. "We got a lot of confidence from it. They laughed at us, but they're not laughing now. They know they were damn lucky to win."

Score by Quarters					
	1	**2**	**3**	**4**	**Total**
Harvard	0	21	7	0	**28**
Penn	14	0	7	6	**27**

Scoring Summary
Penn –   Clune 73 pass from Shue (Startzell kick)
Penn –   Clune 32 pass from Shue (Startzell kick)
Harvard –   Stoeckel 4 run (Tetiriek kick)
Harvard –   Gatto 4 run (Tetiriek kick)
Harvard -   DeMars 1 run Tetiriek kick)
Harvard -   Stoeckel 1 run (Tetiriek kick)
Penn –   Gaetano 11 pass from Shue (Startzell kick)
Penn –   Clune 76 pass from Mandel (pass failed)
Attendance – 21,770

1971: Wild About Harry
Although Penn finished the season with a 2-7 record under new coach Harry Gamble, the games seemed more competitive (except, of course, for the "obligatory" loss to Cornell, in the season finale at Franklin Field). And with a good group of sophomores coming in, hope sprang eternal.

15. Shue Fit

October 28, 1972 - Penn 15, Princeton 10

"When Gary Shue came in, it was just like bringing George Blanda off the bench."

Shue Laces Tigers Up in Knots

*Penn defensive linemen **John Chizmadia** (arms extended) and **Ed Flanagan** apply pressure to Princeton quarterback Fred Dalzell (16). Penn came back from a 10-0 deficit to win.*

"When **Gary Shue** came in, it was just like bringing George Blanda off the bench. He performed like an old pro," said Otto Kneidinger, Penn's defensive coordinator. Indeed, the Quaker coaching staff could not have dreamed of asking for any more miracles than they got from the senior left-hander, who left the bench late in the 3rd period on a rain-soaked afternoon to lead the Red and Blue to its 1st win over Princeton

Franklin Field Saturdays

since 1968. "It's the greatest feeling I've had here at Penn," said Shue, while packing the game ball into his athletic bag. It was also one of the happier moments experienced by Penn football fans in quite some time.

With Franklin Field's AstroTurf becoming drenched, the water-logged Quaker attack was unable to respond to the challenge of a 10-0 Tiger lead. Looking for some spark, Quaker coach Harry Gamble turned to Shue. Just what the doctor ordered. Shue directed the Quakers in touchdown drives of 56 and 48 yards on five for eight passing, to put the Tigers down for good. But Shue was not the only secret weapon whom Gamble decided to unleash. The most unheralded had to be split end **John Downey**. After the Tiger rush dropped Shue twice early in the final quarter, the Quakers had a 3rd and 27 situation on their own 48.

While cries of "Who's that?" floated through the press box (Downey's name did not even appear in the program) the sophomore moved from his wide receiver's spot to take what appeared to be a backward screen pass from Shue. After two steps forward drew the defense toward him, Downey straightened up and threw deep to flanker **Fred McCormick** for 35 yards and a clutch 1st down, setting up the winning score on the next play.

McCormick was fortunate, because the rain seemed to affect everyone on the field. The slippery conditions led to 14 fumbles and four interceptions and held Penn's juggernaut option offense to two yards rushing in the 1st half. The coach deduced that the only recourse was to throw the ball. "We had to get one phase of our game going to loosen them up," he reasoned. "That's why you saw **Adolph Bellizeare** and **Ralph McGee** run so well later on. Actually, the defensive backs have the biggest problems on rainy days when they make their cuts. The football was dried for the quarterback, so throwing wasn't so much a big risk."

Both these points were borne out on the follow-up play to Downey's razzle-dazzle. Shue sent a 3rd unexpected hero, senior **Tom Corbin**, down the sidelines on a "Z and go" pattern. Corbin's last cut put him past his defender, and Shue hit him perfectly in the corner of the end zone for a 17-yard score. The catch, which gave Corbin his 1st touchdown in a Penn uniform, was only the 2nd reception of his career.

The action in the 1st half was by no means as fast, nor as successful, especially from the Quakers' point of view. Safety **Tom Welsh** ended two Tiger threats, once by stealing the ball and once by picking off a pass in the end zone. Play skidded back and forth, however, and a scoreless tie did not appear to be an impossibility, until Princeton scored on a 42-yard field goal in the 2nd quarter for the only points of the half. "The 1st half was just like a three-ring circus," Bellizeare remarked, "but in the 2nd half we made sure these problems wouldn't bother us."

It took a while to turn things around, though, as the Tigers drove 46 yards on their 1st possession for their only touchdown. When Penn didn't move on two more drives, Gamble called on Shue. Eleven plays later, Bellizeare plunged over from one yard out, then sifted into the end zone to pull in Shue's 2-point conversion pass, making the score 10-8. Shue's appearance seemed to have a stabilizing effect on the entire Quaker team: the defense denied Princeton's offense the opportunity to score for the remainder of the contest, and when a Princeton punter let a snap from center get by him, the Quakers simply ran out the clock, taking the Tigers by the tail for the 1st time in four years.

Score by Quarters					
	1	2	3	4	**Total**
Princeton	3	0	7	0	**10**
Penn	0	0	8	7	**15**

Scoring Summary
Princeton –   Bartges 42 FG
Princeton –   Perkins 13 run (Bartges kick)
Penn –   Bellizeare 1 run (Bellizeare pass from Shue)
Penn –   Corbin 17 pass from Shue (Martin kick)
Attendance – 9,285

16. Riding the Wave

November 11, 1972 - Penn 48, Yale 30

"They don't make Homecoming games at Penn like they used to."

Homecoming Treat – Quakers Maul Bulldogs

Quaker halfback **Adolph Bellizeare** (6) gets up a head of steam while starting off on a 50-yard punt return, in the 3rd quarter of Penn's victory over Yale.

"So, at one point, the score stood at 41-0 in favor of Penn. <u>Forty-one to nothing in favor of the University of Pennsylvania.</u> They don't make Homecoming games at Penn like they used to."

Frank Dolson (Class of 1954), Philadelphia newspaper columnist.

Riding a wave, Penn rolled over favored Yale 48-30 before a Homecoming crowd of 21,380 at Franklin Field. The win left the Quakers with a 5-2 record for the year and assured them of their 1st winning season since 1968 (and their 4th in the last 20). Besides marking the 1st time since 1941 that Penn completed a clean sweep of Princeton, Harvard and Yale, the team's 4th win in a row left it in a position to challenge for the Ancient Eight title for the 1st time in 13 years. "Our chances for the title are good," said quarterback **Marc Mandel**. "It's the kind of position we like to be in."

Almost as nice a position as leading 41-0, which is the one the Quakers were in before both teams gave way to their 2nd stringers. The only thing more efficient than the Red and Blue's offensive machine was their defense, which jammed the Bulldogs' high-geared wishbone attack right from the start. Testimony came from an appreciative offense, typified by tackle **Joe Italiano**'s remarks: "They're the bigger team, but we're quicker. The key was getting off the ball and into them quickly." That's certainly what happened in the game's opening series, in which the Elis lost three yards and had to surrender the ball and good field position to Penn, who took full advantage.

"We noticed a glaring opening in Yale's secondary," said coach Harry Gamble. "The coaches spotted it on the 2nd play, and we decided to take advantage of it." That the Quakers did, as Mandel marched the team 41 yards, culminating in a 19-yard slant-in pass to wide receiver **Don Clune** for the 1st score. 7-0, Penn. Next was a flanker-around to **Fred McCormick,** who raced 30 yards for Penn's 2nd tally. 14-0. In the meantime, while Penn's defense was choking off any semblance of a scoring drive by the Bulldogs, **Adolph Bellizeare** scored twice on 2-yard gallops. 28-0. Next, Mandel (35-0), McCormick again (41-0) and **John Sheffield** (48-8) all took trips to the end zone. The Elis scored all 30 of their points in the game's last 18 minutes to even the final stats.

Yale coach Carmen Cozza explained his team's sudden reversal from its 45-14 drubbing of Dartmouth the previous week: "There's no doubt they have a tremendous home-court advantage on the AstroTurf," he said. "This team wouldn't beat us in a month of days by that score on regular turf. We had the same trouble against Cornell with footing. But Penn played a good game, and we couldn't have played worse." Gamble seemed most relieved by the fact that for once he didn't have to sweat out a come-from-behind effort. "We've come from behind so many times, I usually leave the field, with a sigh of relief," he sighed. "The balance of our running and passing attacks helped us today. We had no breakdowns in containing their option, and we played our best football of the year." The victory was Penn's 1st over Yale since 1962.

Score by Quarters					
	1	2	3	4	Total
Yale	0	0	8	22	**30**
Penn	6	21	14	7	**48**

Scoring Summary
Penn – Clune 19 pass from Mandel (kick failed)
Penn – McCormick 3 run (Martin kick)
Penn – Bellizeare 2 run (Martin kick)
Penn – Bellizeare 2 run (Martin kick)
Penn – Mandel 1 run (Martin kick)
Penn – McCormick 3 run (Martin kick)
Yale – Jauron 3 run (Green run)
Penn – Sheffield 1 run (Martin kick)
Yale - Mierzwinsky 1 run (run failed)
Yale – Donohue 1 run (Fernandez pass from Purrington)
Yale – Donohue 1 run (Sortal pass from Purrington)
Attendance – 21,380

17. What Might Have Been

November 25, 1972 - Dartmouth 31, Penn 17

"For of all sad words of tongue or pen, the saddest are these: 'It might have been.'"

42,422 See Quakers Fall in Championship Game

*Dartmouth's Wyman Simmons reaches the crucial Penn fumble ahead of **Ralph McGee** (22).*

"Sometimes when you jump on a duck, you miss it."
Tom Welsh, Penn safety

In the end, a ruptured duck doomed Penn. Dartmouth defeated the Quakers 31-17 in this Ivy League championship game, clinching its 4th straight Ivy title. It was a wobbly, under-thrown pass that turned out to be the most crucial play of the game. The score was tied, 17-17, with less than seven minutes to play, when the Big Green faced a 3rd-and-11 situation on their own 30. Dartmouth coach Jake Crouthamel decided to send in halfback Doug Lind with a pass play. Lind trotted onto the field, but his Dartmouth teammates waved him back. "They took so much time in the huddle that they told me to scat."

Crouthamel was visibly disturbed that Lind didn't make it to the huddle. "I was a little upset," said the Big Green mentor. "We had been penalized a couple times before for taking too much time." So Steve Stetson, the Dartmouth quarterback, went with his own play, a "Z-in" post pattern to halfback Chuck Thomas, the man whom Lind was supposed to replace. Thomas sped down the right side of the field and made his cut inward. Stetson heaved his pass down the middle, a short, bloated, floating pass, a "ruptured duck" that seemed destined for easy interception by a Quaker defensive backs. "1 saw them (the defensive backs) when I made my cut," said Thomas, "but I wasn't thinking of them when I made my leap for the ball."

In a scene reminiscent of the Palestra, Thomas went up for the *rebound,* uh, pass, and totally shocked both the Penn secondary and the 42,422 fans by hauling in the football for 35 yards and a 1st down at the Red and Blue 35. It was more like an interception *by* Thomas than a completion *to* him, and it was the catch of the year as far as the Big Green was concerned. "That was the turning point of the game," said Stetson. "No way that should have happened. Thomas sewed up the game. He just outplayed those defensive backs."

"I didn't know who he (Stetson) was throwing to," said Quaker safety **Tom Welsh**. "I thought it was me. I never saw Thomas. Sometimes when you jump on a duck, you miss it." From there, it took the Big Green six plays to score what turned out to be the winning touchdown. Fullback Steve Webster's 1-yard plunge on 3rd and goal with 3:04 left in the game made the score 24-17, Dartmouth. But it was still too early to break out the bubbly. Following the Dartmouth kickoff, Penn drove assertively to the Big Green 47, where the Quakers faced a 2nd and six situation. Following the snap, quarterback **Tom Pinto** turned to his left but collided with running back **Ralph McGee.** And there went the football... After what seemed like an eternity, Dartmouth linebacker Wyman Simmons finally jumped on the loose ball. On the next play, Big Green running back Rich Klupchak sprinted 50 yards for the game's final touchdown.

Klupchak's run was the climax of an afternoon that saw the Quakers grab a 14-0 lead in the 2nd quarter on tallies by **Marc Mandel** and **John Sheffield**, then lose it as Stetson and Klupchak scored in the same period. Field goals by Dartmouth's Ted Perry and Penn's **Tim Martin** brought the score to 17-17, then Thomas picked off his duck. "We just made too many mistakes," said Quaker coach Harry Gamble. "Our offense was bogged down by a couple of key interceptions, and we had problems with offsides penalties. The mistakes hurt us more than anything else."

Adolph Bellizeare became the 2nd leading single-season rusher in Penn history by gaining 126 yards. The Quakers set new school records for total offense in a season and most rushing yards in a season, and the 263 points scored was the 2nd highest amount in Penn history. Dartmouth became the 1st Ivy league team to win four titles in a row. "It was a good year, there were a lot of sophomores and juniors," said Bellizeare. "Everybody had their ups and downs in the wins and losses. I just think that next year we'll have a hell of a team. The rest of the league won't be confident against us for a long time."

Score by Quarters	1	2	3	4	Total
Dartmouth	0	14	3	14	31
Penn	7	7	0	3	17

Scoring Summary
Penn –   Mandel 8 run (Martin kick)
Penn –   Sheffield 2 run (Martin kick)
Dartmouth -   Stetson 3 run (Perry kick)
Dartmouth -   Klupchak 10 pass from Stetson (Perry kick)
Dartmouth –   Perry 37 FG
Penn -   Martin 25 FG
Dartmouth –   Webster 1 run (Perry kick)
Dartmouth –   Klupchak 50 run (Perry kick)
Attendance – 42,422

Still Believers by Phil Shimkin, *Daily Pennsylvanian*
The ball just sat there. For several agonizing seconds it lay on Franklin Field's AstroTurf in plain view of the 42,422 fans who had flocked to the 33rd Street oval to view the impossible: Penn playing Dartmouth for the Ivy League football title. The Red and Blue had fought the perennial champs to a standstill, but the visitors from Hanover had grabbed a 24-17 lead late in the 4th quarter. With less than three minutes left, the Quakers were driving for a retaliatory touchdown. Then, the fumble. Tom Pinto couldn't get it.

The ball had slipped from his heavily taped right hand after a collision with halfback Ralph McGee, and all the junior quarterback could do was squirm desperately on the green carpet while the pigskin rested a few feet away. "I tried to get up," he said." I tried, but I was facing the other way. I couldn't get up in time." Harry Gamble couldn't get it. The Quaker coach who had instilled the dream of a championship in his players would gladly have flung himself on the fumble, but all he could do was watch painfully from 30 yards away on the sideline. "The ball must have lain there a half an hour," he said afterward. Wyman Simmons, the Dartmouth linebacker, finally spotted the loose ball sitting at midfield and pounced on it. "I saw the fumble, but I thought that they (Penn) would pick it up," he said later. "When I finally broke through and saw it was still there I couldn't believe it." On the play after Simmons' recovery, Big Green halfback Rich Klupchak slanted off left tackle, burst through the stacked Penn line, and outsprinted the Red and Blue secondary 50 yards to the end zone.

Thus ended the Penn dream. The 1st Ancient Eight title since 1959, the same title that had seemed so distant after the 24-20 loss to Cornell on the 3rd weekend of the season, slipped away. Shame it had to end like that. The back-to-back plays would not have been out of place in the disastrous 2-7 1971 season, but they were new to the 1972 campaign. The Quakers had managed to avoid a big mistake for five heady weeks. Maybe they couldn't have kept it up forever. No one could have convinced them of that.

Gamble's "100 percent believers" always felt they would succeed. Even though they lost the Ivy crown last Saturday, they remained confident in their own abilities. The post-game dressing room scene was sad, of course, but it wasn't tragic. Even in defeat, the Quakers retained their winning attitude. "When you're not outmanned, you're not outplayed, and you're not outclassed, you see good things in a game," Gamble said. "We played good football. We had a good year and everybody realizes it." Amen.

It also doesn't seem premature to think that they will have a good year next season, too. Penn football turned the corner this season. Next year the team will count as Ivy title contenders. Gamble's crew will lose valuable leadership from the Class of '73, but the basic ingredients that made this year a success will be back. The only thing next year's squad must be wary of is overconfidence. The Penn team of 1969 and the Columbia squad of 1972 provide historical proof of the danger of that. As long as the Quakers remain 100 per cent believers, they will win. They didn't lose that feeling, despite Saturday's crucial fumble. And that is the important thing.

1972: So Close
For the 1st time in 13 years, the Quakers entered their final game still in contention for the Ivy League title. And for the 1st time since 1941, they beat Princeton, Harvard and Yale in the same season. The Quakers' explosive offensive style was also drawing bigger crowds to Franklin Field. With a final record of 6-3, things were looking up.

18. Homecoming Heartbreaker

November 3, 1973 - Harvard 34, Penn 30

"Impossible things happen when you have faith. Harvard is the greatest place on Earth."

Harvard Hands Penn a Homecoming Heartbreaker

Harvard quarterback Jim Stoeckel rolls away from the pass rush of Penn defensive end **Bob Thomson,** *in Harvard's 34-30 victory over the Quakers, before a Homecoming crowd of 37,167.*

This game was indeed memorable. Between them, the teams made nine fumbles, two interceptions and one blocked punt. On one sequence, they exchanged fumbles on successive plays. But Penn and Harvard rolled up almost 1,000 yards between them, setting seven team and league records. Penn running back **Adolph Bellizeare** gained 138 yards, including a spectacular 67-yard touchdown run for Penn's 1st touchdown.

Receiver **Don Clune** caught 10 passes. Quarterback **Marty Vaughn** completed 18 of 31 passes for 303 yards. Statistically, they all had their best games of the year. However, despite 533 yards of total offense, Penn *gave up* 34 points to the Crimson, so Harvard came away the victor, setting a few records of their own. Enjoying the best day of his career, Harvard quarterback Jim Stoeckel connected on a Harvard record 27 of 48 passes, and as a team, Harvard picked up 456 yards in total offense.

"Stoeckel's done a pretty good job throwing all year," said a disconsolate head coach Harry Gamble after the game, "but I didn't expect him to throw that much, and I didn't expect him to do that well." Even though Stoeckel and company exploited the defense to perfection, they were never able to put the game out of Penn's reach, and with a little over three minutes left in the game, Harvard found themselves down 28-27. Getting the ball at their own 37, three pass plays by Stoeckel were good for a net loss of three yards. Faced with a do-or-die 4th-down situation, the quarterback hit his favorite receiver, Pat McInally, with a perfect strike that gained 15 yards and a 1st down at the 49 yard line. Moving the team with ease, Stoeckel passes gave Harvard a 3rd and three situation at the Penn 30.

The winning score, an almost indescribable catch by McInally, came with 1:26 remaining and Harvard out of timeouts. Stoeckel fired a deep pass as McInally circled in the end zone. As the ball neared the goal line flag, the 6'6" receiver leaped, snatching the ball with one hand and then the other, then fell into the end zone. Penn co-captain and roverback **Jim Bumgardner** offered a non-technical interpretation of the play: "The guy just made a great catch," he said. The score was now Harvard 34, Penn 28. An intentional safety taken by Harvard in the closing seconds made it 34-30, but the game was essentially over after McInally's catch. "Impossible things happen when you have faith.

Harvard is the greatest place on Earth," said McInally after the game *(non-sequitur noted)*.

Before the Crimson's winning drive, the Quakers had made a little comeback of their own, to regain the lead at 28-27. After moving into the locker room at half-time down 21-10, Harvard came out roaring in the 3rd quarter, and scored with only a minute gone to make the score 21-17. Seven minutes later, a 33-yard field goal reduced the Quakers' lead to 21-20. The Penn defense held strong and forced the Crimson to punt the next time it had the ball, but the kick was fumbled by Penn, and Harvard recovered at Penn's 7-yard line. Harvard scored three plays later, gaining a 27-21 lead at the end of the 3rd period.

As the 4th period opened, the Quaker offense came back under the direction of **Marc Mandel**. "I wanted to give Vaughn a rest," said Gamble. After taking a breather, Vaughn reverted to the form he had shown in the 1st half, by hitting Don Clune four times *en* route to a 71-yard touchdown drive. Vaughn was always under pressure when throwing, but now coach Gamble decided to cross up Harvard's defensive wires. Inserting the power-I in what seemed to be an obvious running attempt, Harvard made the expected reaction by stacking five men left of the line.

But instead of handing off the ball on this 4th down and five situation at the Harvard 23, Vaughn floated a perfect pass to halfback **Jack Wixted**, who was 10 yards ahead of his nearest defender. The result was a Penn touchdown and a short-lived 28-27 lead. The Quakers got the ball back one more time but failed to capitalize. Taking over on their own 33, Vaughn threw two quick strikes to Bellizeare and one to Clune. On the next play, however, a Crimson defender intercepted Vaughn's low bomb, intended for flanker **Bob Bucola** near the goal line, sealing the Harvard victory.

Franklin Field Saturdays

Score by Quarters	1	2	3	4	Total
Harvard	0	10	17	7	**34**
Penn	0	21	0	9	**30**

Harvard –   Miller 9 run (Tetiriek kick)
Penn –   Bellizeare 67 run (Martin kick)
Penn –   Kochersperger 8 run (Martin kick)
Penn –   Bellizeare 1 run (Martin kick)
Harvard –   Tetiriek 20 FG
Harvard –   Stoeckel 11 run (Tetiriek kick)
Harvard –   Tetiriek 33 FG
Harvard –   Miller 2 run (Tetiriek kick)
Penn –   Wixted 23 pass from Vaughn (Martin kick)
Harvard –   McInally 30 pass from Stoeckel (Tetiriek kick)
Penn –   Safety – Stoeckel downed ball in end zone
Attendance – 37,167

19. Beep Beep

November 24, 1973 - Penn 31, Cornell 22

"Beep Beep!"

Bellizeare's Runs Lead Quakers over Big Red

*Penn defenders **Pete Sgro** (87) and **Bob Thomson** (70) squeeze off Cornell running back Horace Bradshaw's planned escape route, in the Quakers' 31-22 victory.*

Before a crowd of 24,559, of whom about 15,000 were horn-crazy Boy Scouts (it was Boy Scout Day), the Quakers won a convincing victory over Cornell. The victory left them in a tie for 2nd place, one game behind champion Dartmouth.

The Red and Blue team ended the season in great fashion. This included some unsung players such as center **Bob Jameson** and defensive backs **John Lyons** and **Jim Bumgardner**. Going against all-Ivy middle guard Mike Phillips, game ball co-winner (with **Don Clune**) Jameson didn't let the heralded Cornell lineman near the Penn backfield. "I was psyched out of my mind," said Jameson. "It's a nice way to end. I had my work cut out. He [Phillips] is fast and strong – he's the best I've ever gone against." But Jameson was a little better than Phillips on this day. And free safety Lyons ended his career with two interceptions, while co-captain Bumgardner picked off a Cornell pass deep in Penn territory late in the 4th quarter, to seal the Quakers' win.

Spotlight – "Beep Beep": As seemed to be the case whenever this year's Penn team played, individual and team records fell by the bucketful. Indeed, seven new records went into the books after this game. **Adolph Bellizeare**'s 43 yards rushing put him two yards over the Quaker career mark of 1,553, set by **Gerry Santini** in 1968. While 43 yards isn't a particularly big deal for a runner, especially Bellizeare, on this day the junior made his usual electrifying heroics in the punt-returning department. With the game still scoreless late in the 1st period, "Beep Beep" (a reference to the speed and elusiveness of the *Looney Tunes*' character "Road Runner") received a punt at his own 27-yard line and, avoiding Cornell tacklers left and right, spurted 73 yards down the left sideline for the Quakers' 1st score of the afternoon. He wasn't finished. Unable to move after the ensuing kickoff, Cornell was forced to punt and inexplicably kicked again to Bellizeare. The Penn superstar returned the favor by exploding up the left sideline a 2nd time, in this case for a 48-yard return to the Cornell 15. It took Penn quarterback **Marty Vaughn** two plays to drive the Quakers to a 14-0 lead. After a handoff to Bellizeare went for no gain, Vaughn rolled to his right and hit split-end Clune with a touchdown pass in the right corner of the end zone.

After a Cornell touchdown with 2:24 left in the 1st half (a 35-yard strike to Horace Bradshaw), the Quakers refused to give in to the clock. Throwing three quick completions, Vaughn set the stage for a **Tim Martin** field goal from 37 yards out, his longest ever, which gave Penn a 17-7 half-time lead. In the 3rd quarter, it looked as though Penn might fold. Getting the ball early in the period, Cornell QB Mark Allen rifled through the Red and Blue secondary on the way to a 76-yard touchdown drive, which culminated in a 10-yard scoring run by

Bradshaw. The score closed the Quaker lead to 17-15, and it was crucial that the offense get some points on the board, and quickly.

They did just that. In the space of four minutes, Vaughn hooked up with fullback **Jack Wixted** for two scoring passes, one from 33 yards out and the other from 14 yards away, to make the score 31-15. Completing 17 of 31 passes that day, Vaughn set new Penn season records for yards passing and total offense. Midway through the 4th quarter, Allen made things a little more interesting by registering another touchdown, narrowing the Penn lead to 31-22, and then came back yet again. Starting with the ball at his own 49, three passes and a run put him on the Penn 5. That's as far as he got. Rover-back Bumgardner stepped in front of the next pass Allen threw and raced 44 yards down the left sideline before being pulled down. Then the Quakers ran out the clock. "It was a great way to end the season," said coach Gamble.

Score by Quarters					
	1	2	3	4	Total
Cornell	0	7	8	7	22
Penn	7	10	14	0	31

Scoring Summary
Penn –   Bellizeare 73 punt return (Martin kick)
Penn –   Clune 16 pass from Vaughn (Martin kick)
Cornell –   Bradshaw 35 pass from Allen (Szynalski kick)
Penn –   Martin 37 FG
Cornell –   Bradshaw 10 run (Wierbinski pass from Allen)
Penn –   Wixted 33 pass from Vaughn (Martin kick)
Penn –   Wixted 14 pass from Vaughn (Martin kick)
Cornell –   Starks 53 pass from Allen (Szynalski kick)
Attendance – 24,559

1973: So Close Again…
This year the Quakers again lost only three games, and those by a total of nine points, to finish in a tie for 2nd place. They'd get 'em next year, for sure – wouldn't they?

20. Tiger Trap

October 26, 1974 - Penn 20, Princeton 18

"We could have put them away like a boxer would have, but we didn't."

Quakers Hold Off Tigers' Rally

*Penn's **Bill Petuskey** (76) executes a perfect spike on a pass by Princeton's Ron Beible (12) during the 3rd quarter. Penn survived a 2nd half rally by Princeton, to remain unbeaten.*

Nine minutes into this game, **Marty Vaughn** threw the 25th touchdown pass of his Quaker career, a 9-yard toss to tight end **Ron Kellogg**. Five minutes later, Vaughn hurled his 26th, a 15-yarder to split end **Bob Bucola**. Those two passes gave Penn a 14-0 lead at half-time, and the unbeaten Quakers appeared only a step away from repeating their shutout of the Tigers the previous year. But things didn't quite work out that way.

"We had them on the ropes," said coach Gamble. "We could have put them away like a boxer would, but we didn't." After a glorious 1st quarter, Penn gave Princeton a little breathing room with an offensive letdown and some weak pass defense. The Tigers roared back, and the Quakers were lucky to escape Franklin Field with a 20-18 victory. Penn scored more 1st quarter points against Princeton than it had against any other opponent this year. Yet after obtaining 146 of its 338 yards of total offense in the opening 15 minutes, the Quaker offense stalled, and the defense found itself barely able to hold off Bob Casciola's rampaging Tigers. Only a horrible misplay of Penn kicker **Tim Martin**'s final punt of the afternoon most likely saved the Quakers.

After Princeton broke the Tigers' scoreless streak versus Penn at seven quarters with a 34- yard field goal at 5:07 of the 3rd period, a 49-yard pass put the Tigers on the Penn 5. Three plays later, rushing ace Walt Snickenberger scored his 8th touchdown of the year; and, after an interception of a Vaughn pass late in the final period, Princeton struck again, this time on a 36-yard touchdown pass. With Penn ahead 20-18 and only 1:20 left to play, Tim Martin survived a 10-man rush to get away a soaring punt that sailed 50 yards *in the air*. The Tigers' Tony Carter, standing on his own 19, let the ball roll by him, adding an extra 12 yards to Martin's boot. Penn downed the ball on the 7, and Princeton had its worst field position of the afternoon. A strong pass defense by **Daryl Taylor**, **Jim Sarruda**, **Fred McCormick** and **Don Page** kept the Tigers in a hole the rest of the way and preserved the Quakers' victory.

Prior to all of the above agita for Penn, and between lapses following the 1st quarter, Penn's offensive unit enjoyed some beautiful moments. A picture-perfect drive in the 3rd period, featuring outside runs by both **Adolph Bellizeare** and **Jack Wixted,** ended with a 1-yard touchdown plunge by Wixted at 9:43, for the Quakers' 3rd (and final) score. For Penn, the most pertinent advice may have come from Princeton coach Bob Casciola, who said, after the game: "You can't play half a football game like we did and expect to win." Penn played half of a game against Princeton, and got away with a two-point victory.

Score by quarters	1	2	3	4	Total
Princeton	0	0	11	7	18
Penn	14	0	6	0	20

Scoring Summary
Penn –   Kellogg 9 pass from Vaughn (Martin kick)
Penn –   Bucola 15 pass from Vaughn (Martin kick)
Princeton - Morrison 34 FG
Penn –   Wixted 1 (kick failed)
Princeton - Snickenberger 2 run (Reid pass from Beible)
Princeton – Chamberlin 36 pass from Beible (Morrison kick)
Attendance – 25,317

1974: And Again…
With only two losses this year (both blowouts by Harvard and Yale), Penn earned only 3rd place in the League. Still, not since 1950 thru 1952 had the Quakers strung together three consecutive winning seasons, and not since 1945 thru 1947 had they finished with three consecutive won-lost records of matching quality. Penn defeated Dartmouth two years in a row for the 1st time since 1951, and this year Princeton fell for the 3rd straight time, the 1st time since 1949. Gamble's men were destroying the Penn record book, but the coach still had no championship to show for it.

21. Like They Had Won the Rose Bowl

November 22, 1975 – Penn 27, Cornell 21

"The way everybody's carrying on, you'd think we'd just won the Rose Bowl."

Red and Blue Send Big Red Home Blue

*Penn's **John Mason** (26) carts a 2-yard **Bob Graustein** pass into the end zone far ahead of Cornell's Dave Monahan, for the Quakers' 2nd touchdown in their win over the Big Red.*

Pandemonium broke loose in the home team's locker room after their season-ending victory over Cornell. They yelled, screamed and backslapped, and offering long ovations to the recipients of Saturday's game balls. In fact, the party got so wild, it prompted one member of the season's never-say-die football squad to say, "The way everybody's carrying on, you'd think we'd just won the Rose Bowl."

Well, it may not have been the Rose Bowl at Franklin Field, but the way the Red and Blue came alive in the 4th quarter, it was apparent that for this day, at least, the game meant as much as a Rose Bowl game did to anyone who had ever played in one. Initially, however, between Penn's mental errors and Cornell's ineptitude, it appeared that the 12,000 Boy Scouts in attendance were in for a long afternoon. Early on, the only thing the Quakers could manage for the fans was a **Bob Graustein**-to-**Ron Kellogg** 10-yard TD pass, which was recalled.

It took an interception by linebacker **Mike Welch** to settle down the Red and Blue and start Penn's 1st scoring drive. The junior returned his pick 21 yards to the Cornell 40. Eight plays later, Penn finally had the 7-0 lead it should have had earlier. Graustein said, "We made a lot of errors early in the game. I think we came out a little over-anxious. The seniors wanted to go out winning, and everyone else wanted to win for the seniors." Unfortunately, the touchdown did not end the Red and Blue miscues, as Graustein fumbled on a keeper on Penn's 1st possession after the score. Two plays later, Cornell runs of 33 and three yards resulted in a Big Red touchdown, which knotted the score at seven apiece. Penn, however, was not to be denied.

Graustein immediately marched the Quakers 80 yards in just over two minutes, in a drive highlighted by three more Kellogg receptions. Kicker **Tim Mazzetti**, listed as a doubtful starter, missed the extra point, leaving Penn with a 13-7 half-time lead. The 2nd half opened with excitement for the Quaker fans, when **Bruce Leonetti** returned the kickoff 75 yards, stopped only by a saving tackle at the 1-yard line. Leonetti, who received the game ball along with tri-captain Kellogg, credited the return to his blockers. Graustein scored a touchdown on the next play, but the resulting 20-7 lead did not stand up. Cornell's reserve quarterback, Jay LaRochelle entered the game late in the 3rd quarter, and with the help of another Penn fumble, passed his team to two TD's and a 21-20 lead, in just three and a half minutes. In the last quarter however, Graustein was hot; he marched his Red and Blue team 69 yards for the game-winning drive, ending with another keeper, this time for 13 yards and a touchdown. "We just weren't going to be denied," he said.

So, while Penn hadn't won the Rose Bowl, they won the last game of a long, disappointing and injury-riddled season, a season in which, just as things were beginning to jell, crippling injuries set it back again. But on this final Franklin Field Saturday of 1975, the injuries, etc. were all irrelevant. This was a day for the seniors – and a day on which pandemonium broke loose.

Ted Gilmore

Score by Quarters	1	2	3	4	Total
Cornell	0	7	0	14	**21**
Penn	0	13	7	7	**27**

Scoring Summary
Penn –   Graustein 1 run (Mazzetti kick)
Cornell –   Fanelli 2 run (Szynalski kick)
Penn –   Mason 2 pass from Graustein (kick failed)
Penn –   Graustein 1 run (Mazzetti kick)
Cornell -   LaRochelle 16 run (Szynalski kick)
Cornell -   Hall 14 pass from LaRochelle (Szynalski kick)
Penn –   Graustein 13 run (Mazzetti kick)
Attendance – 21,112

1975: At Least We Keep Beating Princeton
Although the season-ending win over Cornell left the Quakers with only a 3-6 overall record, the team received much praise from both its fans and opponents for its endurance in dealing with countless injuries and bad breaks, its heroics against Cornell and Princeton (for the 4th consecutive year) and its overall team spirit. Harry Gamble signed a new 5-year deal, and fans assumed that winning seasons would resume. With the exception of 1977, they did not. The 1976 team won only three games (including Princeton), and by a total of three points.

22. Tiger Kings

October 29, 1977 - Penn 21, Princeton 10

"Nobody's stopped them in the past month."

Quakers Defeat Tigers for the 6th Straight Time

*Quaker quarterback **Tom Roland** pitches out on this play to **John Mason**, who ran the ball in for a 19-yard touchdown and the game's 1st score.*

"We knew we could roll on them."
Kevin Blake, Penn running back

"One hell of a win," Penn coach Harry Gamble exhorted his team, and no one in Franklin Field's homecoming crowd of 14,696 could have phrased it better. The Quakers, trailing by three at the half, came to life and whipped Princeton, 21-10. "The defense was lying down, especially in the 2nd quarter," Gamble said. "Coach Kneidinger (defensive coordinator) gave a rip-roaring talk at half-time. We knew attitude would win it, and we made no adjustments." It was the Quakers' unprecedented 6th win in a row over the Tigers.

The game started out close, as expected. Both teams moved the ball well, but the only scoring opportunity was a blocked Tiger field-goal attempt. The Penn wishbone, which ground out 331 yards, set a new Penn single-season rushing record with 2,076 yards. Three minutes into the 2nd quarter, **Johnny Mason** took a **Tom Roland** pitch and scooted 19 yards down the sideline for the game's 1st score. Mason, Roland and **Denis Grosvenor** all had impressive runs in the 73-yard drive.

"You can't stop a wishbone if it's executed well, and Penn just executed it beautifully," Princeton coach Bob Casciola offered as a compliment. The Quakers' only offensive problem in the 1st half was not having the ball enough. On Princeton's 1st possession after Penn's touchdown, Tiger quarterback Kirby Lockhart took his team 82 yards to tie the score, as he picked apart the Quaker secondary with short passes to his backs and ends. "We had the feeling Princeton would try to run on us," said Gamble. However, Quaker linebacker **Bob Nix** best explained the reason for the change in the Tiger attack: "They passed because it worked." Princeton drove to another score late in the half, moving the ball from its own 11 yard-line to the Penn 18, setting up a field goal that sent it into the locker room with a 10-7 lead.

A new Quaker team came out for the 3rd quarter. The hard running of Grosvenor (140 yards), Roland (98), and **Kevin Blake** continued to devour the yards as it had done all season. With 27 seconds left in the quarter, Blake capped a 35-yard drive with a 2-yard plunge, putting Penn ahead 14-10. "We heard they were one of the best defenses in the league," said Blake. "But that's because they're not on the field long since their offense eats up the clock. We knew we could roll on them. They weren't doing anything we hadn't seen before."

Although the Penn aerial attack netted zero yards, Princeton was busy enough trying to stop the run. The real story in the 2nd half was the toughening of the Penn defense, as it held the Tigers to just three 1st downs, 33 yards passing and 41 yards rushing. "In the 1st half we were beating ourselves with mistakes," said safety **Mike Daley**. In the 2nd half, a stronger pass rush and a more attentive secondary prevented Princeton from moving the ball. Grosvenor scored Penn's insurance touchdown midway through the final quarter on another long drive. "Penn can play with anybody as long as they don't beat themselves with turnovers," said Casciola, "Nobody's stopped them in the last month."

It *was* one heck of a month for the Quakers.

Score by quarters					
	1	2	3	4	Total
Princeton	0	10	0	0	**10**
Penn	0	7	7	7	**21**

Scoring Summary
Penn –   Mason, 19 run (LeVan kick)
Princeton –   Isom, 2 run (Howe kick)
Princeton –   Howe 35 FG
Penn –   Blake, 2 run (LeVan kick)
Penn –   Grosvenor, 1 run (Perilstein kick)
Attendance – 14,696

1977: At Least We *Still* Keep Beating Princeton

Picked for last place in the Ivies by most prognosticators, this 1977 Penn team was a pleasant surprise to all of its fans and family - finishing in 3rd place with a 5-4 record, which included the above (6th-in-a-row) win over Princeton. With quarterback Tom Roland returning, 1978 looked to be a good year; however, once again injuries and just plain bad luck contributed to a terribly frustrating season. 1979 was even worse, as the team went winless.

23. Finally

October 4, 1980 – Penn 24, Columbia 13

"Losing is a Disease – ah, but curable!"

Losing Streak Finally Snapped

Quakers **Greg Hemmings** *(19)*, **Mike Murphy** *(35)* and **Bob Hailey** *(90) exult after the victory.*

> *"After that 1st series in the 2nd half when we stopped them in 3, we realized we could stop them."*
> **Gary Winemaster**, Penn defensive end

It was over, and it couldn't have happened in a better fashion. "It" was the Quaker football team's 17-game winless, 14-game losing streak, which finally came to a halt at Franklin Field. The Red and Blue overcame a 13-0 half-time deficit to whip Columbia, 24-13. The way things looked at intermission, one never would have guessed that *this* game would end the streak. The Lions scored the 1st time they had the ball and went on to dominate the 1st half. However, after a half-time lecture from coach Gamble, Penn emerged totally different.

The 1st possession of the 2nd half for each team told the story of the game. Penn stopped Columbia in three plays, which it had done only the entire 1st half. "After that 1st series in the 2nd half when we stopped them in 3, we realized we *could* stop them," said defensive end **Gary Winemaster**. Once the Quaker offense got the ball, it started to roll. With quarterback **Doug Marzonie** and halfback **Paul Brodsky** running the ball, the Red and Blue moved 35 yards in five plays, with Marzonie darting to the left for the final 10 yards. With just four minutes gone, Penn had cut the Light Blue lead to 13-7.

As the 3rd quarter ended, the suddenly powerful Quaker attack was clicking with machine-like precision. On the quarter's final play, Brodsky's 5-yard run gave the Red and Blue the ball on the Lion 27. The drive stalled at the 14, and **John Dwyer** came in to boot a 31-yard field goal, narrowing the margin to 13-10. The Quaker defense stopped the Lions cold again, and with 10:50 to play, the Big Quaker Machine roared again. Starting on their own 23, the Quakers went 77 yards in seven plays for the go-ahead score. Running back **Rick Beauvais** took control of the game, cutting the Columbia defense to shreds and eventually bursting downfield for 25 yards to the Columbia 5.

On the next play, Marzonie went into the end zone, and the Quaker side of the field erupted. Columbia briefly showed signs of life after that, but an illegal use-of-hands penalty pushed the Lions backward. Then, on a double reverse, Penn cornerback **Greg Hemmings** caused a fumble, which safety **Tony Liberatore** fell on at the Columbia 44. Then, the "B-boys" (Brodsky and Beauvais) took over, driving downfield to the Columbia 5-yard line again. Brodsky took a pitch from Marzonie and covered the final five yards to give Penn a 24-13 lead with only 2:34 to play. Defensive end **Bob Fleck**'s interception with 1:35 remaining sewed up the Quakers' 1st win since they defeated Columbia, 31-19 at Franklin Field, on October 7, 1978.

Score by Quarters					
	1	2	3	4	Total
Columbia	3	10	0	0	**13**
Penn	0	0	7	17	**24**

Scoring Summary
Columbia –   Cabrera 23 FG
Columbia –   Cabrera 1 run (Cabrera kick)
Columbia -   Cabrera 20 FG
Penn –   Marzonie 10 run (Dwyer kick)
Penn –   Dwyer 31 FG
Penn –   Marzonie 5 run (Dwyer kick)
Penn –   Brodsky 5 run (Dwyer kick)
Attendance – 7,076

1980: End of An Era
The joy of the above win over Columbia did not last long. That was to be the Quakers' only victory of 1980, and Harry Gamble's last hurrah – he resigned at the end of the season. 43-year-old **Jerry Berndt**, previously the head coach at tiny DePauw University in Indiana, was hired to replace Gamble. Some people wondered if coming to Penn was too big of a leap for Berndt.

24. Vura to Hall

September 19, 1981 - Penn 29, Cornell 22

"There's a new sheriff in town."

"Jer-ry, Jer-ry" - New Coach Wins Opener

Penn's **Steve Rubin (20),** *celebrates his TD, reducing the Cornell lead to 22-14 in the 3rd quarter.*

> *"Eight months ago. I said that our 1st goal was to beat Cornell on September 19. And well, we did it. That's not a bad start."*
> **Jerry Berndt,** Penn Head Coach

If you weren't there, you missed one of the most spectacular, dramatic football games that a Franklin Field audience had witnessed in years. You also missed the **Gary Vura**-to-**Karl Hall** aerial display, which spelled three long-distance touchdown passes and a funeral dirge for the wishbone offense. And finally, you missed a man named Jerry

Berndt being carried off the field triumphantly, after leading the Penn Quakers to a down-to-the-wire 29-22 opening-day victory over Cornell, in his debut as head coach. After the game, Berndt said, "Eight months ago I said that our 1st goal was to beat Cornell on September 19." "We did. That's not a bad start." But a lot of sweaty palms and anxious moments preceded Berndt flashing his trademark smile to the throng of reporters and well-wishers after the game. (Read on…)

Coming into this debut game of coach Berndt, Penn had won exactly one game since October 7, 1978. In the 3rd quarter, it appeared that the Quakers were destined to lose again, as the Big Red held a 22-7 lead. But Penn mounted a remarkable comeback, via what was, quite simply, an air show. After years of Harry Gamble's wishbone offense, the Red and Blue took to the sky.

After a 3rd-quarter touchdown pass from **Doug Marzonie** to **Steve Rubin** brought the score to 22-14, in the 4th quarter, on a 2nd-and-10 from the Penn 7-yard line, Vura hit Hall with a long pass in the middle of the field. Hall, running like the great racehorse Secretariat, left the entire Cornell secondary in a cloud of dust, heading for a 93-yard touchdown, the longest touchdown pass play in Penn history. Vura then sped around right end for the 2-point conversion, deadlocking the score at 22-22, with 7:58 to play. Then, with 6:51 to play, Penn got the ball back at the Cornell 48. On 2nd and 22, Vura tossed a 40-yarder to the right of the end zone to Hall, who out-jumped the Cornell safety and came down with both the ball and a 29-22 Penn lead.

Cornell had not yet finished, however. A pass-interference penalty against Penn brought the Big Red to the Penn 1-yard line, with three seconds left on the clock, and Penn's hopes were hanging by a thread. Cornell quarterback Chris Metz took the snap and hustled around left end with two blockers in front of him, when he met up with Penn defensive back **John Waterfield.** Waterfield, who had committed the interference penalty that had put the ball on the 1, hit Metz straight-on, stopping him at the 6-inch line. "I started the final play on the other side of the field," Waterfield said. "I came laterally across, and he (Metz) cut right back into me." For the Quakers, their heroics before 15,871 enthusiastic fans brought them their 1st opening day triumph since 1977. "What a team effort," said Vura, who started the game on the bench. "You couldn't single out one individual." Berndt was hoisted in the air by his players, and the stands erupted in the chant of "Jer-ry, Jer-ry!

The Jerry Berndt Era of Penn football had begun, and with a bang.

Score by Quarters					
	1	2	3	4	Total
Cornell	6	9	7	0	22
Penn	0	7	7	15	29

Scoring Summary
Cornell –   Rubenstein 47 FG
Cornell –   Rubenstein 46 FG
Cornell –   Zittel 1 run (Rubenstein kick)
Penn –   Hall 84 pass from Vura (Shulman kick)
Cornell –   Safety – punt blocked out of end zone
Cornell –   Harmon 9 run (Rubenstein kick)
Penn –   Rubin 7 pass from Marzonie (Shulman kick)
Penn –   Hall 93 pass from Vura (Vura run)
Penn –   Hall 40 pass from Vura (Shulman kick)
Attendance – 15,871

1981: And the Start of a New One

After Jerry Berndt's opening day triumph, visions of sugar plums in the form of an Ivy League title quickly vanished. In their next game, the Quakers were stomped on by Lehigh (58-0), and they did not win another game all year. But *no one* could have foreseen what would happen in the next season.

'Hall'-lelujah! – Karl's Catches Help Usher in the Jerry Berndt Era

*The combination of QB **Gary Vura** (16, top) to wide receiver **Karl Hall** (bottom) clicked for three TD's and 252 yards, sparking the Quakers to a come-from-behind victory over Cornell at Franklin Field.*

25. Curtain Call

October 23, 1982 - Penn 27, Yale 14

"There is a tide in the affairs of men, which, taken at the flood, leads on to fortune."

Red and Blue Team Remains Unbeaten in Ivy, Takes a Bow after Victory

CURTAIN CALL: Responding to chanting from the fans, the Penn football team runs out to greet the crowd after the game - a thrilling 27-14 victory over Yale.

> *"There seemed to be electricity in the air. It seemed like the people were staying in the stands and wanted to see them. We thought this moment would be remembered by these guys for so long, so we let them hang on to it for a little bit longer."*
> **Jerry Berndt,** Penn Head Coach

After all of the game had been played, the final statistics and score entered in the books, and even after the last arm had waved for the singing of "The Red and Blue,' the 1982 Penn football team made a truly great play to cap off an emotional Homecoming contest - it returned to the 50-yard line of Franklin Field. "We thought the moment was right for it to happen," coach Jerry Berndt said in the locker room after he had returned. "There seemed to be electricity in the air. It seemed like the people were staying in the stands and wanted to see them. We thought this moment would be remembered by these guys for so long, so we let them hang on to it for a little bit longer."

It was a moment to remember for both the players and the fans. The football team, having just beaten Yale for the 1st time since 1972 by a 27-14 score, was standing on the turf and listening to those fans remaining (out of the 32,175 total) shout "We're Number One" It was a chance for students, parents, and alumni to show a collective pride in the University. Many alumni who had not seen the Quakers play football for many years had come back for *this* Homecoming game, just to watch their team contend for the Ivy League championship. For the better part of the day and well into the night, the campus was alive with planned receptions and spontaneous celebrations. "A lot of people, especially recent grads, came back to see a winning football team, which they never got to see when they were here," said one alum.

Any returning Pennsylvanians who weren't impressed by the Quakers' sluggish 1st half (Yale led, 7-3) were dancing in the aisles at its conclusion. After **Dave Shulman** kicked a 48-yard field goal to reduce the deficit to 1, **Steve Rubin** scored from five yards out. Next, the Quakers recovered a Yale fumble at the Bulldogs' seven-yard line, and with 14:06 left to play, Steve Rubin ran the ball in again, to give Penn a 20-7 lead. After a Yale touchdown reduced the lead to 20-14 and gave the Penn fans agita, **Tim Chambers** made his 2nd interception late in the game, and **Steve Flacco** iced matters by taking a pitch from QB **Gary Vura** and outracing the entire Yale defense for an 83-yard touchdown. When **Mike Christiani** finished a superb day at linebacker with an interception (the Quakers' 5th takeaway of the game), it was all over but the standing ovation. The win left the Quakers at 5-1 for the season, but at an even more important 4-0 in the Ivy League. Thus, any combination of Penn wins and Harvard losses adding up to three would mean the Quakers would have an Ivy Title of their own. Of course, who knew that three weeks later, like in *Casablanca*, "destiny would take a hand."

Score by Quarters	1	2	3	4	Total
Yale	0	7	0	7	14
Penn	3	0	10	14	27

Scoring Summary
Penn – Shulman 34 FG
Yale – Javens 5 pass from Dufek (Moore kick)
Penn – Shulman 48 FG
Penn – Rubin 5 run (Shulman kick)
Penn – Rubin 7 run (Shulman kick)
Yale – Andrie 2 run (Moore kick)
Penn – Flacco 83 run (Shulman kick)
Attendance – 32,175

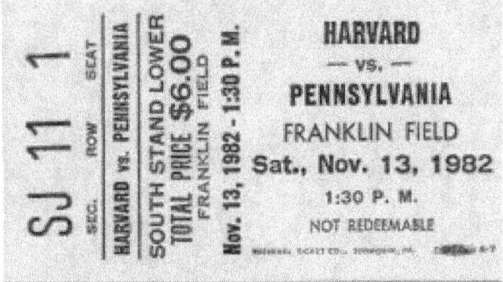

Franklin Field Saturdays

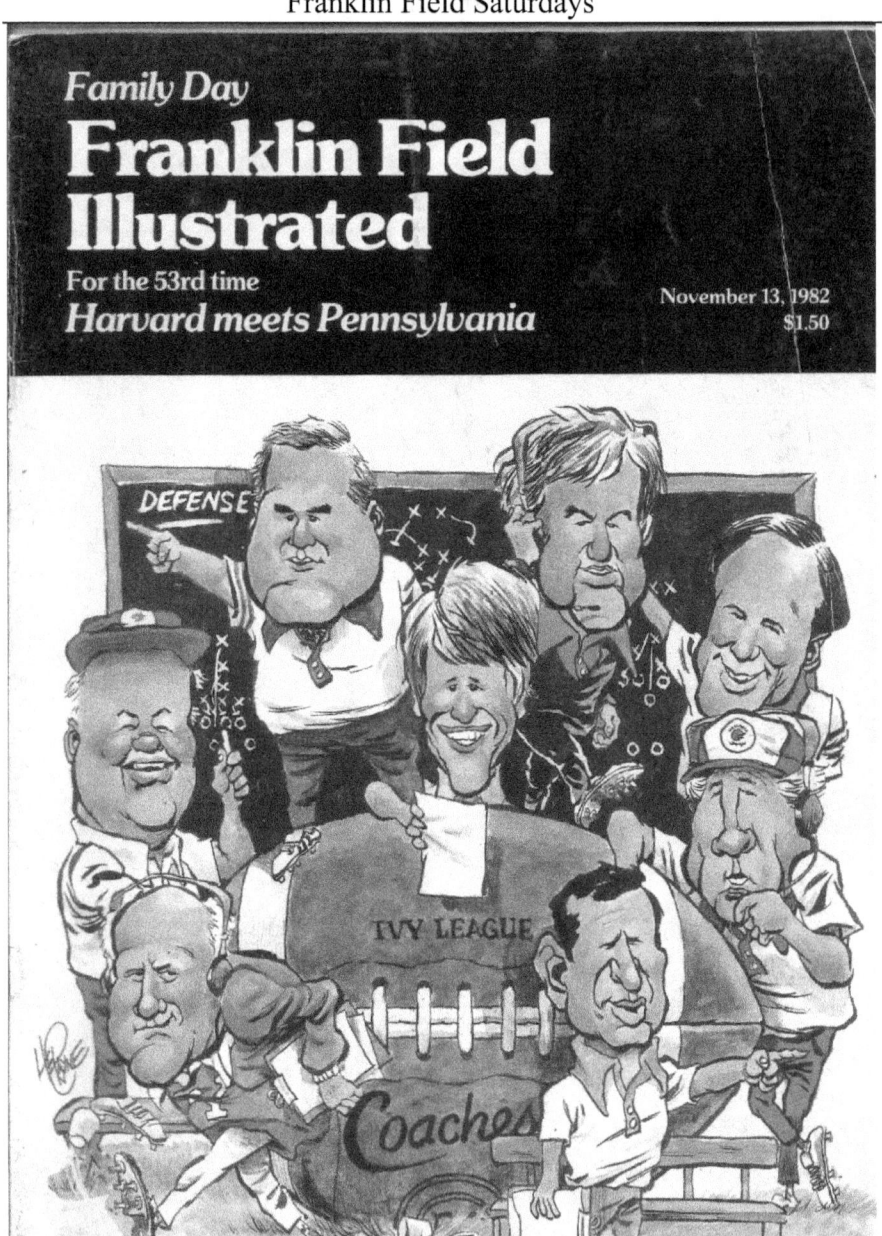

To see why Jerry Berndt (center) is smiling, turn the page...

26. The Miracle on 33rd Street

November 13, 1982 – ~~Harvard 21, Penn 20~~

"It ain't over till it's over."

2nd Chance Field Goal Wins It for Penn

Dave Shulman *(center, bent over) celebrates as his 2nd chance field goal attempt, a 27-yarder, sails cleanly through the uprights. Holder* ***Gary Vura*** *(16) and fans in the background signal the final outcome: Penn 23, Harvard 21.*

> *"After the 1st kick, my heart was down in my toes. I said, 'Oh my Lord, we lost this game.' Then all of a sudden, I saw the flag*

out on the field. It was an incredible feeling to see the flag, to see that we still had a chance to win."
Jerry Berndt, Penn Head Coach

Penn fans will be talking about this game for the next 100 years. Literally making time stand still, the Quakers won an incredible 23-21 victory before 34,876 fans, ensuring themselves of a share of their 1st Ivy League title since 1959. Following a sequence memorable for the emotions involved as much as for what actually happened on the field, the Quakers needed two more plays when there was time for only 1. With 0:03 left on the clock, **Dave Shulman**'s field goal attempt (a 38-yarder) sailed wide to the left as time ran out. Harvard led 21-20, and the Ivy League title appeared destined for Cambridge. But a yellow flag changed destiny. "After the 1st kick, a drained coach Jerry Berndt recalled of the field goal, "my heart was down in my toes. I said, 'oh my Lord, we lost this game.' Then all of a sudden, I saw the flag out on the field. It was an incredible feeling to see the flag, to see we still had a chance to win." It *was* incredible. Harvard was called for running into the kicker and penalized 10 yards. After waiting through Penn's final timeout, they could only watch as Shulman made his 2nd chance count.

The emotion surrounding the finish of the game is difficult to capture. Through three quarters and part of the 4th, the Quakers had treated the Crimson the way the Penn fans ultimately treated the goalposts. When tailback **Steve Flacco** scored from one yard out with 13:19 left in the game, the Quakers had opened up a 20-0 lead, and were so completely in control that the frenzied crowd had every reason to sense a championship.

However, the Crimson came back. First, Harvard QB Don Allard hit tight end Peter Quartararo from the three for the 1st score, and then the Quaker offense suddenly lapsed. When the 1st Penn punt of the day was partially blocked and went only 11 yards, the Crimson struck back again with a 4-yard TD pass. Trailing 20-14 and well into nail-biting time, Harvard got the ball back with 5:04 left. On 2nd down from midfield, Allard threw along the right sideline for John O'Brien, who made a spectacular one-handed grab. The Crimson drove to the 2-yard line with 2:12 left, and Penn stiffened. **Kevin Bradley** stopped Mike

Granger for a loss of two. Allard rolled right and was forced out of bounds al the three. Then **Mike Okun** broke up a pass to O'Brien in the end zone, which set up a 4th-down situation. With Penn's defense getting its biggest chance to test its "we bend but don't break" philosophy, Allard rolled right, drew three defenders, and pitched to Granger, who went in to the end zone untouched.

Harvard converted the extra point, and the Quakers were suddenly fighting for their lives, trailing by 21-20. After giving up the crushing 3rd and final touchdown, what happened in the next (and final) 1:24 was almost too unbelievable to comprehend while it was happening.

The Quakers began their final drive at their own 20-yard line. Quarterback **Gary Vura** had to scramble out of the pocket for one yard. On the next play, he was sacked at the Penn 15. 32 seconds were used up, to go five yards backward. And then things got worse. Vura connected with wide receiver **Rich Syrek** for an 18-yard gain and a 1st down, but finished the play lying woozy near his own end zone. As he was helped off the field, it looked like the Quakers were finally out of miracles. **Fred Rafeedie** came in to throw the ball out of bounds and stop the clock, with 24 seconds left.

But with their backs to the ultimate wall, with their emotional level close to the bottom, the Quakers found a spark. Vura, who had returned to the game, fired the ball over the middle for **Warren Buehler**, at midfield. The ball and the Harvard cornerback hit Buehler at the same time; but instead of falling to the ground, the pigskin popped right into the hands of a trailing Syrek, for a 19-yard gain into Harvard territory. Now some kind of a chance still seemed possible, even if not probable. Vura hit Buehler on the right side with 10 seconds left, for another 16 yards, and then he hit Flacco for 11 yards, to the Harvard 21. There were three seconds left in the game. Jerry Berndt pointed his finger at Shulman. It was time for the Quakers to pull off the Miracle on 33rd Street.

After Shulman's 1st field goal attempt missed, the crowd sat silent, while the Harvard bench erupted. A 2nd emotional trip, this time upwards, began when the penalty flag flew, and the crowd erupted while the Harvard bench took *its* turn being stunned. Then, after Shulman's 2nd kick sailed through the uprights, the celebrating Penn players formed a gigantic blue mass in the middle of the field, and the fans poured out of the stands. It may have been the most exciting finish in Penn and Franklin Field history. The 1st casualty was the west goalpost, which admirers dismantled and dumped into the Schuylkill River.

If there was any guarding of emotion in a locker room that was noticeably less crazy than could have been expected, it was probably because the Quakers realized that their season was not yet over. Several Penn players reminded their teammates about the next week's game at Cornell - they realized that the difference between an outright title and a shared one was still in their own hands. Either that, or the players were just drained. After all, making time stand still was not easy.

Ecstatic Penn fans tear down the west goal post, as the scoreboard tells the story of glory, of "Penn-syl-vay-nigh-yah."

Score by Quarters					
	1	2	3	4	Total
Harvard	0	0	0	21	**21**
Penn	10	0	3	10	**23**

Scoring Summary
Penn – Shulman 27 FG
Penn – Vasturia 9 pass from Vura (Shulman kick)
Penn – Shulman 25 FG
Penn – Flacco 1 run (Shulman kick)
Harvard – Quartararo 3 pass from Allard (Villanueva kick)
Harvard – Ernst 4 pass from Allard (Villanueva kick)
Harvard – Granger 3 run (Villanueva kick)
Penn – Shulman 27 FG
Attendance – 34,876

1982: Beyond Our Wildest Dreams
Unfortunately, and perhaps not unexpectedly, Penn had nothing left in the emotional gas tank for the following Saturday's finale against Cornell, in Ithaca. Before a national TV audience, the Quakers were whipped 23-0, by a conversely fired-up Big Red team, who were saying good-bye to their retiring head coach Bob Blackman. The loss left the Quakers in a 3-way tie for the championship with Harvard and Dartmouth; however, having won their 1st Ivy football championship in *any* fashion in 23 years, *no one* at Penn was complaining.

Recollection from Vahe Gregorian, Class of 1983
I was a seldom-seen receiver on that '82 team, my senior season. Played "left out," I like to say. But that was one of the best days of my life, because of the brotherhood before, during and since that game. We had a lot of rough seasons before that. The varsity had won two games in the previous three seasons, as I recall off the top of my head. And then the turnaround in Coach Berndt's 2nd season. And then a microcosm of it all that day with the incredible comeback, and, of course, the 2nd-chance field goal with no time on the clock after the roughing the kicker penalty. I remember the huge crowd, mid-30,000s, I believe, in part because it was an NFL strike season, but also in part because it had been decades since Penn had had such a meaningful game. When the 2nd kick went through, I was overcome. I remember throwing my helmet in the air, never guessing fans would storm the field. Had to go back and find it, felt lucky it was there. I think we all came out of that game bonded for life in a certain way, all the more so for having shared so much defeat before a joyous moment that still gives me chills.

"The Miracle on 33rd Street" – A Condensed Version

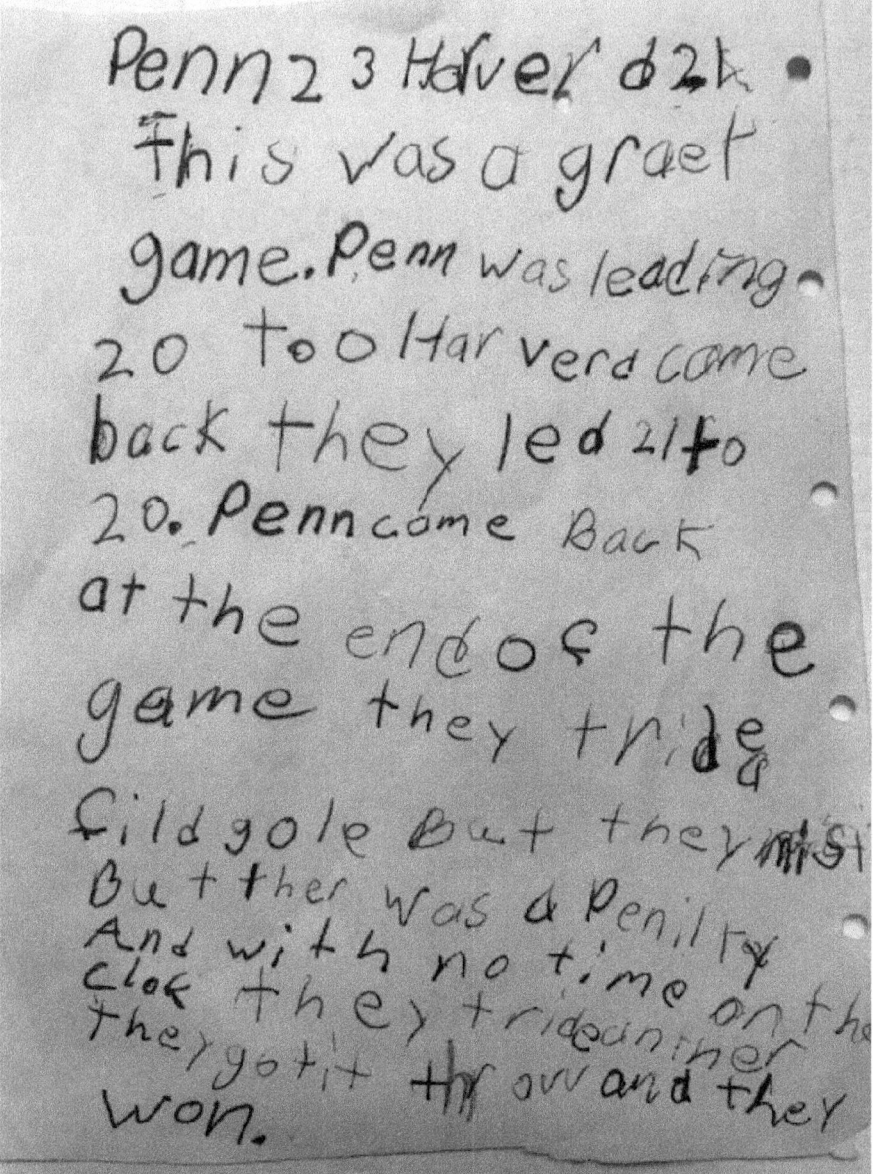

A 7-year-old's eyewitness account of "The Miracle on 33rd Street."

27. Butler Didn't Do It

October 29, 1983 – Penn 28, Princeton 27

"I saw all those people and thought, 'Now is the time.'"

Quakers Stop Two Point Conversion Try at Finish

*Penn defensive end **David Smith**, who sacked Princeton QB Doug Butler on the game's last play, and saved the day for the Quakers.*

On this gorgeous Franklin Field Saturday, a Homecoming crowd of 36,569 people witnessed another Penn-Princeton thriller. Princeton had won five contests in a row in this fabled series, including the previous year's, in which the Tigers were a heavy underdog. Now the Quakers were favored again, but the Orange and Black quickly jumped out to a 14-0 lead, including via a 95-yard touchdown pass and run from quarterback Doug Butler to Derek Graham. Penn quarterback **John McGeehan** and running back **Steve Ortman** brought the Quakers back to tie the game at 14-14, but a 67-yard TD drive by Princeton put the

Tigers back on top at half-time, 21-14. Slowly but surely, the Red and Blue worked their way back: First, a 44-yard 4th-quarter touchdown run by Ortman made the score 21-20 (a 2-point conversion try was missed). After an interception by **Tim Chambers** on Princeton's next series, fullback **Chuck Nolan** scored on a 12-yard run. This, along with a successful 2-point conversion (a **John McGeehan** pass to **Jim O'Toole**) gave Penn its 1st lead of the game at 28-21, with four minutes and 11 seconds remaining in the game.

But Princeton wasn't quite finished yet. Capitalizing on two Penn penalties, the Tigers advanced to the Penn 43; then, on 4th and 12 from the Penn 45, a 21-yard pass from Butler to Devin Guthrie put the ball on the Penn 24. Three more plays netted only three yards, however, and now it was 4th down and seven from the Penn 21, with only 41 seconds left. Not content with just getting a 1st down, Butler went for paydirt, hitting his receiver Graham, who ran the ball in for a touchdown with 31 seconds to go, making the score Penn 28, Princeton 27. Princeton now lined up for the 2-point conversion attempt, which would decide the final outcome of the game. The crowd was in a frenzy. It was at this time that Penn defensive end **David Smith** looked up into the stands, "and I saw all those shakers and heard the crowd. I hadn't had a great game, hadn't done anything spectacular. I saw all those people and thought, 'Now is the time.'"

The ball was snapped and Butler rolled to his right, but he could not find an open receiver. He started to throw, but then hesitated. He never saw Smith closing in. In that moment of hesitation, Smith pounced on Butler and drove him to the ground. The Tiger was dead.

Score by Quarters	1	2	3	4	Total
Princeton	7	14	0	6	27
Penn	0	14	0	14	28

Scoring Summary

Princeton–   Ferraro 20 run (Miskovsky kick)
Princeton –   Graham 95 pass from Butler (Miskovsky kick)
Penn –   Ortman 1 run (Shulman kick)
Penn –   Nolan 6 run (Shulman kick)
Princeton –   Luczak 4 pass from Butler (Miskovsky kick)
Penn –   Ortman 44 run (run failed)
Penn –   Nolan 12 run (O'Toole pass from McGeehan)
Princeton –   Graham 21 pass from Butler (run failed)
Attendance – 36,569

Recollection from John McGeehan, Class of 1985
The Princeton game felt different in 1983. It had a big game feel. And I don't mean the attitude of the team - we had fully "bought in" to the notion that ALL of the games were big, but it seemed like people were all of a sudden paying attention to Penn Football. It was Homecoming weekend. There was a big crowd. And while there was tremendous excitement for the Harvard game in '82, this felt more like we belonged in games like this. We also managed to win (in dramatic fashion, thank you David Smith) in a game in which we didn't play our best. In an odd way it was a confidence builder for us - or maybe just for me?

28. Back to Back

November 19, 1983 – Penn 38, Dartmouth 14

"We've turned it around."

With TV Cameras Rolling, Quakers Roll Over Big Green

"We've turned it around." Jerry Berndt, Penn head coach

This year, it - the title-clinching game - was a lot easier. Compared to the previous year's heart-stopper against Harvard, this was a piece of cake. And Jerry Berndt as always, never doubted, not even in the 1st quarter at Franklin Field, when his team didn't appear concerned with winning the Ivy League title. With national TV Network (ABC) cameras rolling for the 1st time at Franklin Field since 1955, the Quakers gained a grand total of 17 yards in their 1st two series. And punted twice. But that, Berndt explained after Penn had won its 2nd consecutive league championship with a 38-14 win over Dartmouth, was all part of the plan. "We were going to be a little conservative at the beginning," said Berndt, whose Quakers would share the title with Harvard. "We just didn't want to create a turnover situation. We just said we'd go out and dominate up front."

After sputtering on those 1st two drives, everything came together in the 2nd quarter. On the 1st touchdown drive, Penn went 88 yards in 13 plays, scoring on **Chuck Nolan**'s 1-yard burst, to make the score 7-0. "Our offensive line just did the job today," said quarterback **John McGeehan**. "There's no doubt about it, there's no way anyone else can take credit." Then the defense did what it was supposed to. On the 1st play of the Big Green's next series, a hit by Penn sophomore defensive back **Duane Hewlett** caused a fumble, which was recovered by Quaker linebacker **Peter Gallagher** on the Dartmouth 26. Five plays later, **Steve Ortman** took a pitch to his left for Penn's 2nd touchdown. Dartmouth's next series lasted twice as long as the previous one = two plays. A Dartmouth pass was intercepted by nose guard **Joe Lorenc** on the 2nd play, after being tipped by defensive tackle **Tom Gilmore**, and the Penn offense took over again, on the Big Green 31. Again, Penn needed just five plays to score. Again, it was Nolan who scored the touchdown, this time from two yards out. So it was 21-0 at the end of the half.

At the end of the 3rd quarter, it was 31-0, after a **Dave Shulman** field goal and a nine-yard touchdown pass from McGeehan to **Pat Buehler**, capping a 36-yard drive, which was set up by an illegal participation penalty on Dartmouth during a punt return. Penn scored its final touchdown in the 4th quarter on a 29-yard drive directed by **Jim Crocicchia**, after **Ken Coombs** made the defense's 4th fumble recovery. The defense also sacked Dartmouth quarterback Frank Polsinello 10 times, for a net loss of 85 yards.

Dartmouth's two touchdowns came well after the game had been decided. When they scored their 2nd one on the last play of the game, the goalpost in the west end zone had already been torn down. Last year, the crowd did not storm the field until Shulman's field goal had given Penn a 23-21 win over Harvard and a share of the title. This year, the celebration of the championship could begin before the game ended. This year, there was never a doubt. Penn, which went 5-1-1 in the league and 6-3-1 overall, was again a *co*-champion, sharing the crown with Harvard. So Berndt is now thinking about a 3rd championship - an outright one. "Three years ago, our attitude was, 'Let's just survive the game.' But the players believe in themselves now, and that's the whole key - they believe in one another, and what I ask them to do." This year, coach Berndt asked his players to help him establish a winning football tradition. And they did just that.

Score by Quarters					
	1	2	3	4	**Total**
Dartmouth	0	0	0	14	**14**
Penn	0	21	10	7	**38**

Scoring Summary
Penn – Nolan 1 run (Shulman kick)
Penn – Ortman 2 run (Shulman kick)
Penn – Nolan 2 run (Shulman kick)
Penn – Shulman 45 FG
Penn – P. Buehler 9 pass from McGeehan (Shulman kick)
Penn – Heneghan 3 pass from Crocicchia (Shulman kick)
Dartmouth– Viccora 79 pass from Polsinello (Saltzgaber kick)
Dartmouth– Viccora 34 pass from Doherty (Saltzgaber kick)
Attendance – 28,416

1983: It's Official

The above victory over Dartmouth gave the Quakers their 2nd consecutive Ivy championship, this time shared only with Harvard. This was perhaps a more remarkable achievement than the previous year's, in which the Penn team had the element of surprise in its favor. This year's team held no such advantage. In any event, at the moment when the Dartmouth game ended, Jerry Berndt could now say this about the Penn program – "We've turned it around."

Recollection from John McGeehan, Class of 1985

The 1983 Dartmouth game was also critical. Mostly because it came after the worst defeat that we (I) had had on a football field during my time at Penn. Harvard beat us badly that year. I can still easily conjure up the frustration from that day. And, I wouldn't be surprised if the Ivy Football powers might have thought it was the end of an odd little surge from Penn Football. Coming back to beat Dartmouth handily was huge. We confirmed for ourselves that we belonged near the top.

29. Three in a Row

November 10, 1984 - Penn 38, Harvard 7

"That's three years and four goalposts. Not bad. It's great."

Ho-Hum - Quakers' Rout Ensures Share of Ivy Title

Penn players celebrate, after winning their 3rd straight Ivy League title.

For the 3rd straight year, Harvard posed the sole obstacle to a Quaker Ivy League title. The game turned out to be everything every Penn player, coach, and fan could ever want. It was thorough and devastating. Every one of the 38,810 attendees knew which was the better team. Penn won 38-7 and clinched at least a share of the Ivy League crown for the 3rd consecutive year. Penn students showed their appreciation by doing what has become fashionable after fabulous Franklin Field games. They deposited yet another goalpost into the Schuylkill River. For head coach Jerry Berndt, who had resurrected Penn football, there was also nothing but happiness. "Right now, I'm in kind of a euphoric state," he said.

The teams entered into this game with identical 5-0 league records. The stage was set, but no real excitement ever arose. The Crimson ran right through the Quaker defense on their 1st possession, but after that, the game changed - although it took the Quakers a while to get going. The defense held Harvard convincingly, but the offense couldn't manage a 1st down until three minutes remained in the 1st quarter. But on a 2nd down-and-seven, quarterback **John McGeehan** hit **Pat Buehler** with an 11-yard pass, and Penn was on its way. Six plays later, Penn fullback **Stan Koss** darted into the end zone from the three-yard line. The score was 7-7, and the 1st quarter had come to a close. For much of the 2nd quarter, the battle continued - albeit in a sloppy fashion. All Penn got out of the quarter was a 41-yard field goal by **Tom Murphy**. Penn had dominated the quarter, yet led only 10-7 at the half.

It was time for the Quakers to do some damage. Penn's **Steve Ortman**, who earlier in the game had gone over the 1,000-yard mark for his rushing career, got the rout underway. On the opening kickoff of the 2nd half, Ortman dropped the ball, then picked it up and ran right through a hole, untouched, for 92 yards and a touchdown. His closest pursuer was **Tim Chambers**, who escorted Ortman across the goal line, and then tackled him in the back of the end zone, as a slew of Penn players piled on. Penn now led 17-7, and the game was never the same. In the 3rd quarter Penn drove 55 yards, mostly on the ground, with fullback **Mike O'Neill** scoring from the 1. In the 4th, McGeehan threw an 18-yard touchdown pass to Buehler, and the score was 31-7. **Steve Olekszyk**'s 7-yard touchdown run rounded out the scoring, gave Penn its biggest victory margin ever against Harvard, and completed a trifecta of victories over Dartmouth, Princeton and Harvard, which no previous Penn team in history had ever accomplished.

Ted Gilmore

Score by Quarters					
	1	2	3	4	Total
Harvard	7	0	0	0	7
Penn	7	3	14	14	38

Scoring Summary
Harvard –   Vignali 5 run (Steinberg kick)
Penn –   Koss 3 run (Murphy kick)
Penn -   Murphy 41 FG
Penn –   Ortman 92 kickoff return (Murphy kick)
Penn –   O'Neill 1 run (Murphy kick)
Penn –   P. Buehler 18 pass from McGeehan (Murphy kick)
Penn –   Olekszyk 7 run (Murphy kick)
Attendance – 38,810

1984: Winning Outright
Penn traveled to Ithaca the following Saturday and easily defeated Cornell, 24-0, earning the Ivy League championship outright. Its final record of 8-1 was the best since 1947, and its most victories since 1928. Undefeated in Ivy League play, this was one of the finest teams in Penn football history. Said Jerry Berndt, "This is what you want a team to realize – not wins, but to play to its full potential." That is surely what this 1984 team did.

Recollection from John McGeehan
This game ended the notion that we were an upstart. We were good and they were good. There was a ton of emotion in the locker room before the game. A funny little aside is that coach Berndt, a devout and mostly quiet man who I don't ever recall having uttered a curse word, displayed his tie to the team before the game. It was red and blue decorated with a series of little doodles. It was not until you looked closely that you could see the doodles each spelled out "**** Harvard." The text on the tie was not bleeped out.

We came out tight, but when Steve Ortman returned the 2nd half kick the floodgates sprang open. Penn football was here to stay.

Franklin Field Saturdays

The Thrill of Victory

30. Doctor Who

November 2, 1985 - Penn 31, Princeton 21

"The defender hit the ball up in the air. Once he touched it, I could pick it up and run with it."

In Like Flynn – Punt Return Helps Cage Tigers

*Penn receiver **Brian Moyer** celebrates after scoring the touchdown that sealed Penn's victory.*

!@*%$#@)*&%*?!!"
The Penn football fans who were watching this game on TV

The Penn football team used brain, not brawn, to get back its edge, and rallied to defeat Princeton 31-21 in front of a homecoming crowd of

33,479. The win allowed Penn to maintain its one game lead in the Ivy League standings, and was another in a long series of memorable battles between Penn and Princeton. But this one will be remembered more for one incredible play than for the overall game, which was pretty incredible in itself.

The Quakers trailed, 21-0 midway through the 2nd quarter but closed to within 21-14, on the strength of two long touchdown drives flanking half-time. Then their defense stiffened, stopping Princeton on its initial possession of the 2nd half and forcing the Tigers to punt from the Penn 38-yard line. The punt was short and high, and **Chris Flynn**, the Quakers' returner, signaled for a fair catch, allowing the ball to hit at the 14-yard line. Princeton's Eduardo Waite went to down the ball as it took a Penn bounce. But Waite hit the ball up in the air.

Once Waite touched the ball, Flynn knew he could pick it up and run with it. That's exactly what Flynn did, and 79 yards later, Penn was within one extra-point conversion of a tie game. "The defender hit the ball up in the air. Once he touched the ball, I could pick it up and run with it," said Flynn.

Not so fast..

The officials obviously didn't know the rules as well as Flynn did, and they initially decided to bring the ball back to the point where Waite originally touched it. But after a looong discussion/argument with Penn coach Jerry Berndt, the referees reversed themselves, and the Quakers earned their touchdown. After **Ray Saunders** converted, they had their tie as well. "It was a big play to gel the emotions up," Flynn said.

Big play indeed. Princeton's 14 1st-quarter points were the most Penn had surrendered to an Ivy opponent in 1985. The onslaught continued in the 2nd quarter, as Princeton scored again at 8:27. The Tigers appeared to be on the verge of a blowout win when they embarked on yet another foray into Penn territory, towards the end of the half. But **Duane Hewlett** stepped in front of a pass and picked it off. That was the turning point. After the interception, Quaker quarterback **Jim Crocicchia** led the team's longest drive of the season, going 80 yards on six passes, including a 12-yard connection to tight end **Brent Novoselsky** for the score.

Then Penn won the game by scoring 17 points in a 15-minute span of the 2nd half. First came a 1-yard pass to tight end **Scott Scungio**, then Flynn's punt return to tie the game. Meanwhile, the Quaker defense was slamming the door on Princeton. The game-winner was a 29-yard Saunders field goal at 2:33 of the final quarter. The Quakers never let Princeton out of its own territory after that, and a 20-yard Crocicchia touchdown pass to **Brian Moyer** completed the scoring.

Score by Quarters					
	1	2	3	4	Total
Princeton	14	7	0	0	21
Penn	0	7	14	10	31

Scoring Summary
Princeton –   Fitchett 8 run (Goodwin kick)
Princeton –   Fire 44 pass from Butler (Goodwin kick)
Princeton -   Climmons 5 pass from Butler (Goodwin kick)
Penn –   Novoselsky 12 pass from Crocicchia (R. Saunders kick)
Penn –   Scungio 1 pass from Crocicchia (R. Saunders kick)
Penn –   Flynn 79 punt return (R. Saunders kick)
Penn –   R. Saunders 29 FG
Penn –   Moyer 20 pass from Crocicchia (R. Saunders kick)
Attendance – 33,479

The "Doctor Who" Game
PBS television broadcast this game, or at least part of it. To the annoyance of Penn fans everywhere, with 5:43 remaining in the 4th quarter, TV play-by-play man Marty Glickman announced that due to the length of the game, the cameras were leaving Franklin Field. TV viewers would not get to watch the end. Instead, at 4:00 p.m., the science-fiction show "Doctor Who" took over the Philadelphia airwaves. Other PBS stations ran "The David Susskind Show." Fortunately, unlike the NFL's infamous "Heidi" game in 1968, no more scoring occurred.

31. Four in a Row

November 23, 1985 - Penn 19, Dartmouth 14

"This is the greatest. You can't ask for more than this, to win four straight championships."

Quakers Mow Down Big Green for 4th Straight Title

Tom Gilmore *(79) reacts after sacking Dartmouth quarterback Brian Stretch.*

In a fitting conclusion to the 1985 football season, Penn defeated Dartmouth 19-14, before 19,802 at Franklin Field, ending the season as began: as undisputed Ivy League champions. After Harvard lost at Yale, the Quakers kept the championship trophy in Philadelphia for the entire next year. Thanks to clutch performances by a host of players not accustomed to the spotlight and the stellar play of their defense, the 1985 Quakers ensured their place in the school's record books by wrapping up an unprecedented 4th consecutive Ivy title. "This is the greatest," co-captain **Tom Gilmore** said after a typically All-American performance that ranked as one of his most inspired ever. "You can't ask for more than this, to win four straight championships. Hardly anyone can say that they did that. It says that we're the best team in the league for four straight years."

In truth, the game was somewhat ugly, but it was gloriously vintage Jerry Berndt, i.e., winning, and winning ugly if necessary. "This game was an example of what our program is all about," said Berndt. "When the time comes, we ask all of our players to be ready." Berndt was speaking about fullback **Mike O'Neill**, 3rd string tailback **Jim Bruni** and backup quarterback **Scott Morcott**. "Their time came up, and they were ready."

Pressed into workhorse duty because of injuries, O'Neill seemed to relish the role and even scored the game-clinching touchdown on a four-yard run in the 3rd quarter. Bruni picked up the rest of the slack, rushing for 87 yards, including 39 in a game-clinching 48-yard drive at the end of the 3rd quarter.

Morcott guided Penn on both of its touchdown drives. The 1st, which came after **Duane Hewlett** recovered Dartmouth's fumble of the opening kickoff, took only 42 seconds and covered only 13 yards. **Rich Comizio** ran three times to eat up the ground, with the last carry being a 5-yard jaunt for the score. Right before half-time, Dartmouth went on an 80-yard drive to tie the game up at 7-7. Other than that drive, Dartmouth struggled all day long to move the ball against a rugged Penn defense.

"We knew we weren't going to lose," said Penn safety **James Fangmeyer**. This was due largely to Penn punter **Dave Fassnacht**'s clutch punt placements, which forced the visitors to start from their own

12, 20 and 25-yard line in the 1st half, and from their two and 16-yard lines in the second. One punt in particular changed the complexion of the ball game. Trying to operate from their own 2-yard line after a 39-yard boot midway through the 3rd quarter, the Big Green collided with Penn's swarming, stunting defense. **Jeff Fortna** burst through Dartmouth's offensive line and buried Dartmouth quarterback Tim Duax in the end tone for a safely and a 9-7 lead, with 8:13 left in the quarter.

It was the way that QB Scott Morcott finished, however, that meant the most to Penn, as he directed the Quakers to their final, game-clinching touchdown. Without a single pass attempt, the Quakers drove to a touchdown that came with 2:51 left in the 3rd quarter. Penn tacked on a 19-yard **Ray Saunders** field goal with just over four minutes remaining, for insurance. They almost needed it when, with 1:20 left in the game, the Quakers' punt coverage broke down, and Dartmouth returned the kick for a 79-yard TD. But that was the Big Green's last hurrah. So call it an ugly victory, but for the 4th straight year, the water level of the Schuylkill River rose on Franklin Field's final football Saturday, as fans ceremoniously buried the east end zone's goalposts in the river. On a day when they admittedly played a sloppy game offensively, the Quakers still found a way to win. And that was their trademark ever since Jerry Berndt arrived on the scene in 1981.

Score by Quarters					
	1	2	3	4	Total
Dartmouth	0	7	0	7	14
Penn	7	0	9	3	19

Scoring Summary
Penn – Comizio 5 run (Saunders kick)
Dartmouth – Michel 25 pass from Gabianelli (Saltzgaber kick)
Penn – Safety, Fortna tackled Duax in end zone
Penn – O'Neill 4 run (Saunders kick)
Penn – Saunders 19 FG
Dartmouth – Truitt 79 punt return (Saltzgaber kick)
Attendance – 19,802

1985: Dynasty
After winning four Ivy titles in a row, the latter two outright, Jerry Berndt moved on, taking the head coaching job at Rice. Quaker fans were concerned about the dynasty continuing, as who could possibly replace him? Shortly thereafter, **Ed Zubrow**, one of Berndt's assistants, was named as the new head coach. Penn fans needn't have worried…

Franklin Field Saturdays

32. (On the Way to) Five in a Row

November 15, 1986 - Penn 17, Harvard 10

"The way that we came out in the 3rd quarter was a key,"

Quakers Hold off Crimson to Set up Title Showdown

*Penn's **Rick Inskeep** (left) and **Bruce McConnell** combine on one of the Quakers' eight sacks of Harvard quarterback Tom Yohe.*

> *"We talk a lot about how important the 1st drive of the 3rd quarter is on both sides of the ball, and how important it is to the football game overall. We scored the 1st two times out in the 3rd quarter, and stuffed them on their 1st possession. Thank goodness we did."*
> **Ed Zubrow**, Penn head coach

This game exemplified why football is played in halves - because these two halves were about as opposite as possible. Defense dominated the 1st half – only three points were scored, which occurred when Penn's **Jim Grass** booted a 25-yard field goal in the 2nd quarter. The half's only other highlight was a 24-yard run by Penn's **Chris Flynn**, which gave him Penn's single season all-purpose yardage record, formerly held by **Adolph Bellizeare**. But, as if a large alarm clock had sounded over Franklin Field at half-time, the 2nd half resembled some of the more memorable contests that the Quakers and Crimson have often played. Both teams moved the ball up and down the field, amassing over 300 yards in total offense in the half, and putting 24 points on the scoreboard between them.

Although Penn played only about one quarter of good football on this day, they won, 17-10, remaining unbeaten on the season. The win by Penn and by Cornell (vs Columbia) set up a head-to-head matchup for the Ivy title in Ithaca, NY. It would be the 1st time since 1968 that two unbeaten Ivy teams would meet to determine the Ivy champion on the final weekend of play. The teams' execution and performance of the two teams in *this* game was less than stellar. Each team lost two fumbles, and Penn threw two interceptions, the 2nd of which made the 25,650 fans in attendance *very* nervous. (Back to that later).

Leading the way on offense for Penn was tailback **Rich Comizio**, who rushed for 132 yards and scored both of Penn's touchdowns. On the Quakers' 1st play from scrimmage in the 2nd half, he went down the left sideline for 41 yards, and the Penn single-season rushing record held by **Gerry Santini** since 1968 (880 yards) was his. Comizio's total of 942 yards also left him only 58 yards away from becoming the 1st running back in Quaker history to rush for 1,000 yards in a season. Five plays after that scamper, Comizio crashed through the right side of the end zone for Penn's 1st touchdown, making the score 10-0.

"The way that we came out in the 3rd quarter was a key," Zubrow said. "We talk a lot about how important the 1st drive of the 3rd quarter is on both sides of the ball and how important it is to the football game overall. We scored the 1st two times out in the 3rd quarter and stuffed them on their 1st possession. "Thank goodness we did." The Quakers would score again later in the quarter. Taking the ball on its 20-yard line, Penn went the 80 yards in eight plays, culminating with Comizio's rumbling in from the 3. The big play was a 42-yard completion from **Jim Crocicchia** to tight end **Brent Novoselsky** that moved the ball to the Harvard 12. Penn led 17-0. Then the fun started:

On the 1st play following a 30-yard field goal by the Crimson, cornerback Don Heberle intercepted Crochiccia at the Penn 41, then returned the ball to the Quaker 20. Four plays later, on 4th down and seven from the 17, Harvard quarterback Tom Yohe found wingback George Sorbara in the end zone for a touchdown. Now it was 17-10, and visions of the 1982 game between these two teams danced through the minds of all.

The Crimson got one last chance. Taking the ball with 7:25 to play on their 31, Yohe drove the Crimson to the Penn 41. On 3rd down and 8, Harvard backup quarterback David Landau entered the game for the 1st time – as wingback. The coach wanted Yohe take the snap and pitch the ball to Landau, who would promptly fire it back to Yohe. But the play never materialized because Quaker defensive tackles **Mike Lista** and **A.J. Sebastianelli** met Landau and dropped him for a 13-yard loss. Yohe's 4th-down pass was incomplete, and Penn iced the game after that. The Quakers were on their way north to Ithaca.

Score by Quarters					
	1	2	3	4	**Total**
Harvard	0	0	0	10	**10**
Penn	0	3	14	0	**17**

Scoring Summary
Penn –   Grass 25 FG
Penn –   Comizio 5 run (Grass kick)
Penn –   Comizio 3 run (Grass kick)
Harvard –   Maretz 28 FG
Harvard –   Sorbara 10 pass from Yohe (Maretz kick)
Attendance – 25,650

1986: How Do You Follow a Legend?
By going 10-0 in your 1st season, that's how. After this victory over Harvard, Ed Zubrow's undefeated Quakers traveled to Ithaca to play the also unbeaten Big Red of Cornell. In frigid conditions, with snow piled around the perimeter of the field, Chris Flynn sealed the tough 31-21 victory with a brilliant 32-yard TD run in the 4th quarter. This win completed a 10-0 season, Penn's 1st perfect record since 1904. The 10 wins also included a 30-26 win over Division 1 Navy, at Annapolis; Penn had not beaten a non-Ivy Division 1 team since 1953.

33. No Taunting, Please

October 10, 1987 - Penn 38, Brown 17

"Let sleeping dogs lie."

"Keys" to Victory = Bruin QB Taunts, Defense

*Sophomore Penn tailback **Bryan Keys** ran for 126 yards, including a 68-yard touchdown run, to lead the Quakers to a 38-17 victory over Brown.*

"That [taunting by Brown QB Mark Donovan] bothered me. That was just fuel to the fire."
Parker Rhode, Penn linebacker

Brown quarterback Mark Donovan was feeling pretty good. He had just pulled off a nifty little bootleg play, and he was about to score untouched from the Penn 6-yard line. The Bruins took a 14-0 1st-quarter lead over the Quakers on their 1st sustained drive of the game. Their previous touchdown had come on a 4-play, 22-yard series after blocking a Penn punt. Donovan himself helped make sure it would be Brown's *only* long drive of the day.

As he crossed the goal line, Donovan decided to taunt the Quakers by waving the ball in their faces. His Bruins had a 2-touchdown lead with over four minutes left in the 1st quarter, and the Quakers seemed doomed to a long afternoon. "That really bothered me," said Penn linebacker **Parker Rohde,** the Quaker closest to Donovan on the play. "That was just fuel to the fire." It also upset Brown head coach John Rosenberg, whose words to Donovan when he came off the field were "Too soon."

"I just don't like that kind of thing," Rosenberg said. "I don't like it, and we don't do it. It's not our nature. But it was an unusual circumstance, and he was so excited that he did it." Said Donovan, "I don't regret what I did; I've done it before, and I'll do it again."

Penn defensive tackle **Mike Lista** thought that Donovan's actions definitely helped wake up the Quakers. "Yeah, I'm sure," he said. "But [their] scoring was enough for me. That was plenty. They were getting pretty cocky out there." Penn head coach Ed Zubrow felt that just the fact that the Bruins appeared to be on their way to beating the Quakers should have been enough to rouse his team. "If looking at the scoreboard doesn't motivate you, then the fact that some kid's waving the ball in your face shouldn't motivate you anymore," Zubrow said. "They put 14 quick points on the board; you've just got to look at the scoreboard to get you motivation back."

Whatever motivated Penn, down 17-0 early in the 2nd quarter, the yield was a ferocious resolve. **Bryan Keys**' 62-yard kickoff return set up **Jim Grass** for a 28-yard field goal, the 1st of 3. Then, **Chris Flynn**'s 7-yard run capped a 11-play, 62-yard drive, and Grass' 40-yard field goal on the final play of the half cut the Bruins' lead to 17-13. Midway through the 3rd period, the Quakers drew closer on Grass' 27-yard field goal, making it 17-16. The Quakers took a 24-17 lead on **Jim Bruni**'s 3-yard plunge and a two-point conversion with four seconds left in the quarter.

Even after essentially finishing off Brown, Penn managed to score twice more. Solid blocking set up a 68-yard touchdown run by Keys in the 4th quarter, as he cut right and then moved back toward the center of the field and outraced the Brown defense, to expand the Quakers' lead to 31-17. Keys would also score the Quakers' final touchdown on a 1-yard plunge. On the afternoon, Keys rushed for 126 yards on 11 carries and two touchdowns, caught one pass for 31 yards, and returned two kickoffs for 80 yards, all in the 2nd half.

Back to the defense. Said linebacker Lista, "It took us until about the end of the 1st quarter to get all our adjustments in. After we did that, we shut them down. We knew during the week from watching films that if we put pressure on Donovan, any kind of pressure near him, he'd fold. That's what we set out to do, and we finally started turning on the heat. It got a little too hot for him." Penn sacked Donovan six times, forcing him to fumble three times. The Bruins could manage just six 1st downs and 112 yards of total offense, after going ahead 17-0. "Defensively we were just going out there trying to shut them down and get the ball back into the offense's hands," Lista said. "As long as we kept them off the board, we were going to be happy. And we did."

Score by Quarters	1	2	3	4	Total
Brown	14	3	0	0	17
Penn	0	13	11	14	38

Scoring Summary
Brown –   Simone 17 pass from Donovan (Kos kick)
Brown –   Donovan 6 run (Kos kick)
Brown –   Kos 39 FG
Penn –   Grass 28 FG
Penn –   Flynn 7 run (Grass kick)
Penn –   Grass 40 FG
Penn –   Grass 27 FG
Penn –   Bruni 3 run (Miklos pass from Keller)
Penn -   Keys 68 run (Grass kick)
Penn –   Keys 1 run (Grass kick)
Attendance – 27,253

1987: Outlier
For the 1st time in six seasons, Penn did not win the Ivy League title. Injuries to too many key players (including quarterback **John Keller** and running back Chris Flynn) and a heartbreaking last second loss to Yale doomed the Quakers to their 1st losing season (4-6) since 1981. However, with Flynn back in the season finale at Franklin Field vs Dartmouth, Penn rolled to a 49-17 victory, and, thanks to the running of emerging sophomore back Bryan Keys, the future looked bright once again.

34. Sweet Revenge

November 12, 1988 - Penn 52, Harvard 13

"There was a tear running down my face as I left the field."

Penn Regains Share of Ivy Title

*Penn safety **Tom Charters** (35) lunges toward Harvard halfback Tony Hinz, in the Quakers' 52-13 annihilation of the Crimson.*

After a year-long absence, at least half of the Ivy League crown returned to Philadelphia. Penn's 52-13 victory over Harvard at Franklin Field, in front of 37,612 fans, guaranteed that to the undefeated Quakers. "What more could I ask for in my final home game," Penn co-captain **Tom Gizzi** said. "Nothing could be more perfect. There was a tear running down my face as I left the field." The Quakers wrested their 6th league title in their last seven years from the defending champions, with enough vengeance for last year's (31-14) loss for two titles. The 39-point advantage was Penn's largest margin of victory in the 109 years the teams have battled. The game ranks as one of Harvard's worst beatings ever. "We played as hard as we could, putting the pressure on, hoping Harvard would crack, and that's exactly what happened," said Penn head coach Ed Zubrow.

Seams in the Crimson defensive line appeared on the Quakers' 1st offensive play. Running back **Bryan Keys** ran 34 yards into Harvard territory to initiate the 1st of Penn's eight scoring drives. The gain moved him past **Chris Flynn** into 2nd place on the Quakers' all-time season rushing list. Keys finished the game with a career-high 178 yards on 28 carries, to join **Rich Comizio** as Penn's only 1,000-yard rushers in a season. Keys rushed for three touchdowns, while quarterback **Malcolm Glover** ran for two and passed for one more. Glover opened the scoring with a 7-yard sprint up the middle, six plays after Keys' 34-yard dash, to put Penn up 7-0.

The Quakers' 2nd drive of the opening quarter notified the Crimson that Penn could move the ball at will. If Harvard's ineffective defense didn't get the message, then Glover's 22-yard touchdown pass to **Dave Whaley** four plays later drilled the point home. Harvard's only good drive of the game came in the opening minutes of the 2nd quarter, which Harvard quarterback Tim Perry concluded with a 3-yard TD scramble, to cut Penn's lead to 14-7.

The Quakers managed only three points in the 2nd quarter, on kicker **Rich Friedenberg**'s 39-yard field goal, and the half ended with Penn leading, 17-7. "There was concern at half-time," said Keys. His concern heightened on Penn's 1st possession of the 2nd half, as Harvard picked off Glover's 1st pass. Glover vindicated himself just 30 seconds later, however, after Penn free safety **Tom Charters** recovered a Crimson fumble on the Harvard 12. "That fumble was the big one," Crimson head coach Joe Restic said. "We lost momentum and field position." And any chance of winning the game.

On the next play, Glover scrambled 10 yards to his left for his 2nd touchdown, and Penn led, 24-7, two minutes into the 2nd half. Six minutes later, Keys slid into the end zone, untouched, from the 3, and the Quakers, ahead 31-7, reveled in the offensive massacre. "We were enjoying sweet revenge," Keys said. Harvard's only other score came early in the 4th quarter, long after the game had been decided. Penn's win set up a championship match against Cornell, in the season finale at Ithaca. A Penn victory would give it the Ivy title outright; a loss, and they would have to share the title with the Big Red.

Score by Quarters					
	1	2	3	4	**Total**
Harvard	0	7	0	6	**13**
Penn	14	3	14	21	**52**

Scoring Summary
Penn –   Glover 7 run (Friedenberg kick)
Penn –   Whaley 22 pass from Glover ((Friedenberg kick)
Harvard –   Perry 3 run (Hall kick)
Penn –   Friedenberg 39 FG
Penn –   Glover 10 run (Friedenberg kick)
Penn –   Keys 3 run (Friedenberg kick)
Harvard –   Reidy 1 run (pass failed)
Penn –   Keys 3 run (Friedenberg kick)
Penn –   Keys 6 run (Friedenberg kick)
Penn –   Maley 1 run (Perry kick)
Attendance – 37,812

1988: Champs Again, But…
After the above blowout victory over Harvard, the unbeaten (9-0) Quakers headed up to Ithaca for the season finale against once-beaten (in the Ivies) Cornell. The favored Penn team seemed poised for its 2nd undefeated season in three years. But it wasn't to be. Penn held a 6-3 lead midway through the 3rd quarter and was threatening to blow the game open. But a 16-point, 4th-quarter explosion by the Big Red denied the Quakers their outright Ivy championship. With the 19-6 Cornell victory, Penn and Cornell finished as co-champs, each with 6-1 league records.

Shortly after the season ended, Penn head coach Ed Zubrow announced that he was leaving the coaching world to work in other endeavors in education. Penn replaced him with former assistant coach **Gary Steele**. Steele's 3-year (1989-91) record at Penn would be 9-21. At the end of the 1991 season, **Al Bagnoli** replaced Steele, and as they say, the rest is history.

35. Ivies on Notice

October 31, 1992 - Penn 13, Yale 10

"If you come to a fork in the road, take it."

Quakers Send Message to Rest of Ivies

*Penn tailback **Sundiata Rush** celebrates after the Quakers' 13-10 victory over Yale at Franklin Field.*

"I think people are going to take notice. Yale is a quality football team. I think it sends a message that we can compete. It was a real good win for our kids."
Al Bagnoli, Penn head coach.

At the start of the 1992 season, no one thought to include Penn among the Ivy League football elite. But, with their 13-10 victory over Yale on a soggy Franklin Field, the Quakers made it clear that they had arrived. "I think people are going to take notice," said coach Al Bagnoli. "Yale is a quality football team. I think it sends a message that we can compete. It was a real good win for our kids." Although the Quakers' win was not pretty; it exemplified what good teams do: take advantage of opportunities. While Penn never truly established any continuity, picking up only eight 1st downs all game, it came up with enough big plays to win.

The Quakers needed such a big play for their 1st score of the game. Following a Yale punt into the wind, the Quakers got the ball on the Eli 41 to open the 2nd quarter. Senior running back **Sundiata Rush** (25 carries, 132 yards) got the handoff, ran right, then cut back left against the over-pursuit. Sprung by a tremendous downfield block by **Tony Hernandez**, Rush darted into the left corner of the end zone to score. But Yale came right back and took the ball down the field in a drive that characterized Penn's defense for the 1st three quarters. The Eli moved the ball from their 27, through a series of runs by quarterback Steve Mills and running back Keith Price. The drive stalled on the Quaker 31, but Mills completed a 24-yard pass on 4th and 10. It was the 1st of three 4th-down conversions for Yale. Penn made a solid goal-line stand, however, and forced the Bulldogs to settle for a field goal. This narrowed the Quaker lead to 7-3, midway through the 2nd quarter.

The goal-line stand foreshadowed a strong Quaker defensive effort in the 2nd half. Following an early 2nd half interception, Yale took a 10-7 lead on a 4-yard touchdown run by Keith Price. But before the Eli were even finished celebrating their touchdown, the Quakers had the ball back deep in Yale territory. **Ako Mott,** making a dazzling 74-yard return, toted the ball all the way to the Yale 12-yard line, and ignited the homecoming crowd of 17,893 in the process. But, instead of taking the ball into the end zone for the go-ahead score, Penn managed to lose 14 yards on its next three plays. On 4th and 24 from the Eli 26-yard line, the Quakers faced a difficult field-goal attempt to tie the game; however, despite facing a stiff head wind, junior kicker **Andy Glockner** made the 43-yarder with room to spare.

The complexion of the game seemed to change immediately after the kick. The Quaker defense got a "kick" of its own, and rose to another level. No longer was Yale able to convert on long 3rd- and 4th-down situations. No longer were the Eli able to confuse the Quakers with option runs. In the final 23 minutes, Penn allowed a paltry 37 yards while collecting five sacks. The Quaker offense continued to have problems, however, and had to rely on another big play to move into position to secure victory. In the last minute of the 3rd quarter, sophomore **Terrance Stokes** dashed for a 37-yard gain to take the Quakers to the Yale 30-yard line. Penn moved the ball only five more yards, but Glockner nailed another field goal, this one a 42-yarder, for the winning score. Offensively speaking, it was not pretty, but there was no question as to who was the better team on this day.

Score by Quarters					
	1	2	3	4	Total
Yale	0	3	7	0	10
Penn	0	7	3	3	13

Scoring Summary
Penn – Rush 41 run (Horowitz kick)
Yale – Swartz 26 field goal
Yale – Price 4 run (Swartz kick)
Penn – Glockner 43 FG
Penn – Glockner 42 FG
Attendance – 17,893

1992: We Have Seen the Future, and Its Name Is Bagnoli
Al Bagnoli's 1st year as head coach was a marvel, as the Quakers exactly reversed their (2-5) Ivy record of the previous season, finishing up at 5-2 (7-3 overall), which earned 3rd place. Not only that, but they were competitive in their two losses, which were against the two top contenders, Princeton and Dartmouth. Penn fans could not wait for next year.

36. Youth Must Be Served

September 18, 1993 – Penn 10, Dartmouth 6

"Today was just our day."

Quaker "Green" Backs Stymie Big Green

Penn players show their jubilation after the horn sounds and their 10-6 victory over 3-time defending Ivy League champion Dartmouth is complete.

Penn disposed of 3-time defending Ivy League champion Dartmouth in regal fashion, and without 40 of its own (Penn's) players. That's right – the Quaker freshmen were ineligible to play on this day, because it was orientation week at Dartmouth, which prevented the Big Green's frosh from playing also.

Jim McGeehan's 166-yard passing effort moved him into 10th place on the Quakers' all-time passing list with 1,923 yards. **Miles Macik** had seven catches, including some big 3rd-down receptions. On the defense, defensive back **Kevin Allen** turned in a rookie-of-the-week performance, intercepting one pass and breaking up four others. Allen had to defend against not only (All-Ivy Dartmouth QB) Jay Fiedler's potent arm, but also his own case of "butterflies," understandable for a first time starter. However, regardless of the stellar individual performances and the final score, the game itself was far from perfect, much like the weather. Intermittent rain and slick field conditions severely hampered Fiedler's passing game, and the home team collected an astounding 11 penalties for a total of 100 yards.

The Quakers handled the weather better than the Big Green, and Fiedler openly admitted his difficulties with the conditions. "If it's raining, it's raining for both sides, but I think the footing hurt me a lot, about as much as the wet ball," said Fiedler, who fumbled two snaps and slipped numerous times. Penn got on the board first, thanks to a 42-yard field goal by senior **Andy Glockner**. Then with 2:09 left in the half, McGeehan pitched right to junior tailback **Terrance Stokes**, who cut through traffic for a 19-yard touchdown run.

With the extra point, the Quakers were leading the defending champs 10-0 at the half. Although Penn failed to score again, it kept Dartmouth in check, as Fiedler connected for only a single score: a 39-yard touchdown pass to Andre Grant. While Mother Nature may have served as Penn's 5th defensive back, the play of the regular four was the story of the day – the play of this inexperienced unit shone brightly, and the aforementioned Kevin Allen shone the brightest of all.

Score by Quarters					
	1	2	3	4	Total
Dartmouth	0	0	0	6	6
Penn	0	10	0	0	10

Scoring Summary
Penn   Glockner 42 FG
Penn   Stokes 19 run (Horowitz kick)
Dartmouth   Grant 39 pass from Fiedler (kick blocked)
Attendance – 13,488

Penn's 'Green' Defensive Backs Shut Down Big Green's Top Gunslinger
by Adam Steinmetz, *Daily Pennsylvanian*

Stopping Dartmouth quarterback Jay Fiedler has proven to be a daunting chore for Ivy League defenses under the best of conditions. Containing Fiedler with two sophomores starting in the secondary figured to be as futile as trying to nail Jell-O to the wall. Fiedler, after all, was the 1992 Ivy League Player of the Year and a 3rd-team Associated Press All-American. He led the entire country (Division I-A and 1-AA) last season in passing efficiency. The Washington Redskins sent scouts to Franklin Field Saturday to observe this Ivy League quarterback.

So it's hard to blame Penn cornerback Kevin Allen and free safety **Sheldon Philip-Guide** for having a few jitters before seeing their 1st varsity action on Saturday. For if cornerbacks are alone on an island, free safeties are in charge of the rescue boats. "If you just looked around the locker room [before the game], myself and Sheldon Philip-Guide, we were wrecks," Allen said. "We were bouncing off walls. Then you look at the older guys like [senior strong safety] **Jimmy Magallanes**, he was calm. Allen was composed after the game and could laugh about the pregame butterflies. His interception with 3:25 remaining should have sealed the Penn win. When the Quakers missed a field goal to give Dartmouth one more chance, Allen broke up a crucial 1st-down pass to help halt Dartmouth's futile final series. Allen, the Ivy League Rookie of the Week, broke up four passes and tallied three tackles to lead the secondary. "Experience was a factor at the beginning of the game," Allen said. "After the 1st couple of plays when you get going and everybody starts hitting, then it evens out."

The young Penn secondary made the crucial plays when it counted most. With 3:44 left and Penn leading 10-6, Fiedler decided to pick on Allen again. Fiedler had tested Allen much of the afternoon with some success, but this time Allen was ready. On 1st down, Allen broke up a pass intended for David Schearer. Fiedler went to work on Allen again the next play and paid the price with an interception.

"Most of the time Dartmouth likes to run the No. 1 receiver on a post, and the No. 2 receiver back outside," Allen said. "I think Fiedler thought I was going to try to stay with the outside man, and he tried to force the ball inside, and I was able to make the play." The entire secondary made the plays on Dartmouth's final possession. On 1st down Allen gambled on a quick-out pattern. It appeared as if Allen charged the ball too late, but he raced toward the ball and broke up the pass. On 4th down Fiedler had plenty of time to pass, but nobody was open. Eventually the pass rush buried Fiedler, and the fans could rejoice in the rain.

And while the professional scouts left with questions about Fiedler, the Penn secondary departed Franklin Field having answered its critics. Just ask Kevin Allen. "I still think he is a good quarterback," he said. "Today was just our day."

Recollection from Jim McGeehan, Class of 1994
Going into the game and season, Dartmouth was the 3-time consecutive Ivy Championship team with the reigning MVP of the league, QB Jay Fiedler, returning. Coach Bagnoli instilled in his players the idea that it was business as usual and everyone had a job to focus on.

It rained all day prior to the game and most of the morning of the game, and let up just prior to kick-off. A wet ball was going to be a factor. QBs do not like playing with wet footballs, particularly on turf. So, during our Friday practice, I worked on gripping a wet ball so that I could feel confident, throwing passes. I had to be prepared, regardless of conditions.

We did not play a particularly good offensive game, but we made critical plays that kept us on the field and kept Dartmouth off. The key was that we held an offensive possession advantage for close to 10 minutes. We controlled the clock. We put Dartmouth in passing situations when our defense was able to line up and get after the QB. We had the best defense in the league, full of ballers, and Dartmouth was not as well prepared for the weather conditions as we were.

Recollection from Miles Macik, Class of 1996

The '93 Dartmouth game was the spark that began two years of dominance in the Ivy League. Looking back, Dartmouth was the best team we played all year. The rain and wind played a big factor. But I think we would still have beaten Dartmouth that season regardless of the week or the weather. We knew we were playing a good football team, and once we figured out that we could handle them, the confidence kicked in, and there was no looking back.

It's important to remember that the 1993 season marked the end of freshman football in the Ivy League and the 1st year that freshmen became eligible to play varsity. This meant that as much as half our roster was playing college football for the 1st time.

The '93 team capitalized on a perfect blend of senior leadership and impressionable young players. Seniors like Dave Betten, Chris Brassell, Jimmy McGeehan, Jim Magallanes and Frank Cacurro had a chip on their shoulder, believing it was "their time." They were hungry, and they made younger players like me believe this team was underestimated and disrespected. The younger guys adopted that mentality, starting with the Dartmouth game.

We had eight to 10 players in their 1st year of eligibility who started or contributed significantly in the game, including Bill Glascott, Kevin Allen, John Scott Freeman, Sheldon Phillup-Guide, Matt Tonelli and Tom McGarrity. I know I was more confident after that game. And I think the younger guys gained a ton of confidence, not just in the win, but in realizing we could compete with and beat any team we played that year. And that's exactly what we did for the next nine weeks.

37. The "~~Keith Elias~~ Terrance Stokes" Game

November 6, 1993 - Penn 30, Princeton 14

"Pride go-eth before a fall."

Elias 'Stokes' the Flames, & Quakers Douse the Tigers

Penn tailback **Terrance Stokes** *(22) runs for daylight during his 42-carry, 272-yard performance, in the Quakers' win over Princeton. 35,810 fans saw the Red and Blue beat the Tigers for the 1st time since 1988.*

"I didn't feel like I got started today. I never felt like I got into a groove. It just didn't pan out for us."
Keith Elias, Princeton running back

"I didn't feel tired at all. Forty plus carries definitely surprised me. I guess a guy my size isn't supposed to carry the ball 42 times."
Terrance Stokes, Penn running back

Keith Elias may still say that he has never regretted his incendiary remarks about Penn's admission standards, which he made in the week leading up to this game between the undefeated Quakers and his unbeaten Tigers. But over the years, for Penn fans, anyway, this game became "The Keith Elias Game." However, it really should be called "The **Terrance Stokes** Game."

The Penn tailback ran for a Penn record 272 yards on 42 carries (7 of which went for 10 or more yards), and in the process, he dissected a soft Tiger defensive front. A strong Red and Blue defense held Elias to just 59 yards on 15 carries. Stokes' actions spoke much louder than Elias' words. In the most anticipated game played at Franklin Field in more than five years (given the Ivy championship implications), Penn lived up to its most important challenge and defeated Princeton 30-14, before a packed homecoming crowd of 35,810. In the process, the Quakers erased a 4-game losing streak against Princeton. Although the unbeaten Quakers still had two extremely tough opponents standing between them and the Ivy title, Penn on this day recaptured the championship spirit that it had lacked for a few years. The energy culminated in zealous fans charging onto the field following the final gun and ripping down the west goalpost.

In addition to Elias' less than stellar performance, the Tigers suffered from an inability to hold onto the football. They fumbled eight times, losing the ball on four of these occasions Penn's good fortune and Princeton's woes began on the game's opening possession. Under overcast skies and a slight drizzle, the Tigers received the ball 1st and started at their own 25-yard line. After gaining a 1st down, quarterback

Joel Foote fumbled the snap, and Penn's **Dave Betten** recovered at the Princeton 41.

Penn capitalized on the Tiger turnover in big-play fashion. On just the 3rd play of the drive, quarterback **Jim McGeehan** found wideout **Chris Brassell** in the far corner of the end zone for a 30-yard strike and a Quaker touchdown. Kicker **Marc Horowitz**'s extra point made the score 7-0, just 1:44 into the game. Another costly Foote fumble off of a snap ended what might have been a Princeton scoring drive, when linebacker **Andy Berlin** recovered the ball at the Penn 18-yard line. Penn then rumbled 82 yards downfield. The 13-play drive hit paydirt when Stokes took the ball in from seven yards out on a 3rd-and-goal situation. Penn now led 14-0.

After the teams traded punts, Princeton got on the board. The Tigers executed a lightning-quick drive that covered 49 yards in just four plays, spanning 55 seconds. On a 2nd-and-goal from just inside the Penn 1-yard line, Tiger fullback Peter Bailey took the handoff up the middle and went untouched into the end zone for the Tiger touchdown. The score was 14-7. Princeton never got closer. Penn put the finishing touches on a good 1st half with another long-yardage drive. Starting deep in their own territory at the 11-yard line, the Quakers put together a 7-play, 89-yard drive, scoring when McGeehan again hooked up with Brassell in the end zone from eight yards out. The 2nd half saw Penn unable to get the ball into the end zone. Instead, the Quakers settled for field goals and were rewarded by the consistent foot of Horowitz. With field goals of 22, 23 and 27 yards, Horowitz enabled the Quakers to maintain a comfortable lead and keep Princeton down and gasping for air.

Penn fans, coaches and players got a scare late in the game when McGeehan, hit late on a scramble play out of bounds, was knocked unconscious. He sustained a concussion, but returned to the field for the sentimental final play. But it wasn't scoring, fumbles, sacks or late hits that kept the crowd on the edge of their seats during the 2nd half. It was Stokes, who, by the middle of the 3rd quarter, had already gained over 200 yards. "I didn't feel tired at all," Stokes said. "[Forty plus] carries definitely surprised me. I guess a guy my size isn't supposed to carry the ball 42 times." Stokes and the Quakers now sat alone atop the Ivy League. For the 1st time in a long while, they controlled their own title destiny.

But the long winding road hadn't quite come full circle yet. "Right now we're in good shape," Bagnoli said. "We can't get too high in victory or too deep in despair. It's not like this was the season-ending victory, and we can hang up our cleats and say, 'This is great.' We enjoyed today, and tomorrow we're back at work."

Score by Quarters					
	1	2	3	4	Total
Princeton	0	7	7	0	**14**
Penn	7	14	3	6	**30**

Scoring Summary
Penn –   Brassell 30 pass from McGeehan (Horowitz kick)
Penn –   Stokes 7 run (Horowitz kick)
Princeton –   Bailey 1 run (Hogg kick)
Penn –   Brassell 8 pass from McGeehan (Horowitz kick)
Penn –   Horowitz 22 FG
Princeton –   Ross 29 pass from Foote (Hogg kick)
Penn –   Horowitz 23 FG
Penn –   Horowitz 27 FG
Attendance – 35,810

Recollection from Terrance Stokes, Class of 1995
November 6, 1993, will forever have special meaning to me. Not because of the individual success I experienced, but because it was a day that Penn football regained respectability in our league. When two undefeated, nationally ranked programs meet so deep in the season, it is an extremely meaningful game. We were coming off a good win at Yale the previous week and were looking forward to this challenge. The coaches made certain that we approached this game in the same manner we approached the previous seven. We knew not to get too high or too low. In fact, the coaching staff never allowed us to realize how well we were playing or how good we actually were. We continued to practice as if we were winless. Princeton was the last team to have

defeated us. Princeton, the top-billed team in the league at the start of the season, featured a nationally recognized player. We were a team of hard working, selfless individuals who were hungry to gain respect, and respect came by winning.

By the time Saturday rolled around, we were completely dialed in. Homecoming festivities did not matter. Which alumni attended did not matter. The only thing that mattered was beating Princeton. In the game itself, we clicked in every phase. Our defense did their job, shutting down what Princeton wanted to do and causing them to turn the ball over. Special teams executed by helping us control field position. Our offense showed how versatile it really was. We had two outstanding receivers for whom Princeton game-planned, so why would they need to game-plan to stop a 160-pound running back? Our offensive coaches noticed this early and were sure to call plays to make them pay. I remember taking advantage of what the defense gave us. My success would not have been possible were it not for the multitude of weapons we had on offense and the outstanding work of the offensive line.

Recollection from Jim McGeehan, Class of 1994
Another rainy weekend, so the turf was soaked. I was prepared for these conditions by now.

Princeton knew we were the best offense in the league and extremely balanced, since we had the best passing attack in the league, and we were just shy of being the #1 rushing offense. Their defensive strategy this game was to focus on stopping the pass with nickel coverage, and Terrance Stokes, the best back in the league that year, made them pay for it. We succeeded early with throwing, which prevented Princeton from changing their game plan. Penn simply outclassed Princeton.

The final score was much closer than the game. We should have won by 40 but had way too many penalties. Princeton was ill-equipped to manage a wet turf, and our defense punished their running backs.

I think what was most embarrassing for Princeton that day is that they came into game as if it were a "friggin war," per their mouthy running back during a pre-game video, while we considered it as simply the next game on the schedule.

Recollection from Miles Macik, Class of 1996
There is so much to remember from this game.

First, the obvious: Terrance Stokes: 42 Carries, 272 Yards. Unbelievable performance that I was proud to watch and be a part of.

Second, the "hype". Of all the games I played in at Penn, this was by far the most hyped, with two 7-0 teams located so close to each other, playing the game that would decide the Ivy Championship.

Third, I remember our 1st series on offense, because Princeton lined up in a completely new defensive formation. Right away, we knew that we were dictating what Princeton was doing on defense and that we could get in formations and create opportunities in the run game for Terrance to get to the 2nd level. From there, we just watched him do the rest.

I think Terrance's individual accomplishments that game are a great example of why the 1993 team was so special. Each week we adjusted. One week it was the pass, and the next it was the run. Some weeks we needed Jimmy's arm and others we needed Terrance on the ground. Some weeks I was the match-up problem for the secondary, and others (like Princeton 1993) it was Chris Brassell. Somehow, in '93, whomever we needed to be the "guy" was always ready and always answered the call. When Terrance got that call against Princeton, he took it to a whole different level. By far one of the best performances I've ever seen, by one of the toughest teammates I've ever had.

38. The 100th Meeting

November 20, 1993 - Penn 17, Cornell 14

"To end on this note makes your life more enjoyable for years to come."

Perfect Quakers Defeat Big Red to Cap 10-0 Season

Exuberant Quaker fans dump an upright off the South Street Bridge into the Schuylkill River, after storming Franklin Field and tearing down the west goalpost.

In this 100th meeting between Penn and Cornell, the Quakers turned the ball over four times in the 1st half, *en* route to a 14-0 deficit, and the Schuylkill River appeared safe from a 2nd date with the goalposts. Penn didn't lead until senior **Marc Horowitz** booted a 30-yard field goal through the uprights with just 5:44 remaining. The kick left the game in the hands of the Penn defense, exactly where Cornell quarterback Bill Lazor had been all afternoon. The Quakers had sacked Lazor nine times with their marvelous defensive ends **Dave Betten** and

Michael "Pup" Turner as ringleaders. Now Cornell was starting its final possession from its own 24, facing a long field and long odds.

The Big Red had not achieved a 1st down in any previous 2nd-half possessions. In the 3rd quarter, they had gained zero yards. But nothing had been easy for Penn fans all afternoon, as a chilly wind blew hats around like hot dog wrappers. Now they would have to endure Cornell's last-gasp drive. In five plays, the Big Red had moved to midfield. Then Lazor hit Ron Mateo on the right side for a 21-yard gain. With two minutes remaining, the Big Red faced a 3rd down and five from the Penn 24. Lazor scrambled for an apparent 1st down, but the refs flagged Cornell for illegal procedure. The penalty set up a 3rd down and 10. After an 8-yard gain, Cornell faced 4th and two from the Penn 21.

A scant 59 seconds remained. Bouncing off two Cornell blockers, Betten grabbed the leg of Big Red running back Chad Levitt and pulled him down. However, from the bottom of the pile, he couldn't see or hear if he had stopped Levitt. But he needn't have worried. Together Betten and lineman **Kelly Tolton** had stopped Levitt one yard short of the 1st down, and the 17-14 Penn victory, undefeated season and 1st Ivy League title since 1988 were preserved. When Betten saw his teammates dancing, he relinquished his hold on Levitt's leg – a memory that he and his teammates could hold forever. "I cannot imagine a better or a more befitting way of going out," said senior quarterback **Jim McGeehan**, trying to hold back tears. "To end on this note makes your life more enjoyable for years to come."

This win did not come easily for the Penn *players*, either. Before 22,618 attendees, in the 1st quarter a Penn fumble set up a 37-yard Cornell touchdown drive, and late in the 2nd, cornerback Terry Golden returned an interception 33 yards to put the Big Red up 14-0. In the 2nd half, however, the Penn defense turned the game around. Junior free safety **Nick Morris** was the "booster rocket" that propelled the Quakers' comeback. With the offense still struggling early in the 3rd quarter, Morris intercepted a Lazor pass near midfield and returned it to the Cornell 29. Three plays later, freshman **Aman Abye** was in the end zone. In the 4th quarter, the offense finally worked out its problems.

Penn opened the quarter with an 86-yard march that tied the game at 14 with 10:19 left. McGeehan capped the drive by hitting **Miles Macik** for a 17-yard touchdown. The Quaker defense then stymied the Big Red again, forcing Cornell to punt for the 12th time. The 21-yard kick into the wind gave Penn the ball on the Cornell 37, and the Quakers drove to the Cornell 13 to set up Horowitz's winning kick.

The Quakers now had bragging rights over other Ivy teams for a full year, and the seniors had bragging rights for life.

Score by Quarters					
	1	2	3	4	Total
Cornell	0	14	0	0	14
Penn	0	0	7	10	17

Scoring Summary
Cornell – Mateo 14 pass from Lazor (Rodin kick)
Cornell – Golden 33 interception return (Rodin kick)
Penn – Abye 4 run (Horowitz kick)
Penn – Macik 17 pass from McGeehan (Horowitz kick)
Penn – Horowitz 30 FG
Attendance – 22,618

1993: Just Awesome
Referring to Cornell's 14-0 half-time lead in the final game of the season, quarterback Jim McGeehan said, "We always have a guy every game who steps up. That's why this team is so good. This team just does not panic." They didn't panic in this one either, and the win gave Penn its 8th Ivy title and an unbeaten season.

Penn vs Cornell - "The 100th Meeting"

Penn players celebrate with the Trustees Cup.

Recollection from Jim McGeehan, Class of 1994

Going into the "100th Meeting" game, after we had broken the Harvard Hex the week before (Penn had not won at Harvard since 1972), winning and ensuring Penn at least a share of the Ivy Championship presented yet another hurdle for this team.

We were on an extreme high going in, but what we learned from our coaches was that we still needed to conduct business. We needed to focus and adjust, again. We had to come back from 14-0 deficit at half-time. And we did. It was not pretty, but we were not a pretty team. We were a determined team. 10 and Oh - Perfect Season. I cannot imagine a better or more befitting way of going out.

39. One Shining Moment

November 12, 1994 - Penn 33, Harvard 0

"They also serve, who only stand and wait."

Chico is "The Man," as Quakers Clinch Title

Terrance Stokes *again rushed for 100 + yards (143, to be exact) in his final game at Franklin Field, as the Quakers clinch sole possession of the Ivy League title.*

In one of their more dominating performances of their remarkable 1994 season, the Penn Quakers thrashed Harvard 33-0, to clinch the Ivy championship for the 2nd year in a row. The win was Penn's 20th straight, the longest current winning streak in the nation. It tied Holy

Cross' all-time Division I-AA record for consecutive victories. In a frenzied locker room after the trophy presentation, the coaches and players were thinking of nothing except Ivy League title No. 2. "Last year, we were just so excited about getting there. I think this year, we just appreciate doing it and how hard the accomplishment is," said coach Al Bagnoli.

As difficult as the accomplishment may have been, this game could not have been easier. After putting up 33 points at Princeton in the previous week, the Quakers matched that performance. Senior **Terrance Stokes** ran wild in his final Franklin Field game, gaining 143 yards on the ground. Quarterback **Mark DeRosa** threw for 170 yards and two touchdowns and directed two long drives for scores before exiting with an injured right thumb in the 3rd quarter. DeRosa 1st led Penn on an 85-yard drive that took 14 plays, including a Stokes scamper from three yards out, to give the Quakers the only points they needed all day.

On the other side of the ball, the Penn defense was its usual swarming, ferocious self, converting six Crimson turnovers into 17 points. Late in the 1st half, in the midst of a desperate attempt to get something going, Penn senior co-captain **Michael "Pup" Turner** separated Harvard QB John Kezirian from the ball. Senior safety **Nick Morris** recovered the loose ball and returned it eight yards to the Harvard 25, with 32 seconds remaining. Three plays later, wide receiver **Miles Macik** drove the dagger into the Crimson's heart. Leaping over two defenders to snag a DeRosa pass, Macik increased Penn's lead to 17-0 with a 19-yard touchdown reception. It was the 122nd reception of his collegiate career, an all-time Penn record. If any doubts remained about the outcome of the game, they dissipated when the Quakers took the 2nd-half kickoff and marched 72 yards for a 23-0 lead. DeRosa capped the drive with a 16-yard strike to senior wide receiver **Leo Congeni**. Soon thereafter DeRosa injured his thumb and had to leave the field, but the Quakers did not stumble when their backup came in. **Steve Teodecki** was 7-for-9 passing, including the touchdown that finished the scoring. He also led Penn to a field goal. With Penn up 23-0 at the end of three quarters, the 4th stanza was simply a grand celebration for the seniors.

Spotlight: Chico Is "The Man." The Quakers finished the scoring with the play-of-the-day: a 22-yard throw from Teodecki to receiver **Mike Chico**, a seldom-used senior who had never caught a pass. Chico's teammates mobbed him after he crossed the goal line. Moments later, the goal posts succumbed to the mob of fans, and the Penn team savored the moment for the 2nd year in a row.

Score by Quarters	1	2	3	4	Total
Harvard	0	0	0	0	**0**
Penn	0	17	6	10	**33**

Scoring Summary
Penn – Stokes 3 run (Glockner kick)
Penn – Glockner 43 FG
Penn – Macik 19 pass from DeRosa (Glockner kick)
Penn – Congemi 16 pass from DeRosa (kick failed)
Penn – Glockner 34 FG
Penn – Chico 22 pass from Teodecki (Glockner kick)
Attendance – 28,918

Chico Finally Gets His Moment in the Sun by Adam Rubin, *Daily Pennsylvanian*
When Mike Chico entered the end zone long after the game and another Ivy title had been decided, teammate **Brian Higgins** began to cry. Chico, a senior playing his last home game, deserved the touchdown. It was his 1st collegiate catch. Now, nearly a half hour after the students had swarmed the field and the players smoked cigars, Chico sat in the interview room at Franklin Field for his 1st and last time, clenching the ball under his right arm. "I'm not letting go of this one," he said.

Whether he was talking about the ball or the moment was unclear. Chico has practiced with the Quakers for four years. He did not see action the last two seasons, and as a senior has received little playing time. The sparse minutes remaining behind Penn's most talented receivers go to underclassmen, who can benefit the program in future seasons.

But Chico has no regrets. He holds no grudges. "I just got caught up in a numbers game," he said. "I understand what the coaches did. I'm a senior with not much experience. Why not play the other guys and get them ready?" That did not lessen the disappointment of what he thought would be a more productive senior season. He spent a lot of time in the weight room and joined the track team last year in part to get in shape. It did contribute more to the euphoria surrounding the only catch he may ever make. Mike Chico just wanted one more chance.

The game had been decided, the fans had begun to assemble for the ritual storming of the field, the Ivy title was a lock. Just one chance. That's all he wanted. Then there was the fumble. It was a meaningless fumble. "This could be it," he thought. The score was 26-0. Three minutes, 46 seconds remained. The huddle, like any after a change of possession, was on the sideline. The 1st play – "Curl Chico, 1st option." "They're calling this play for me," he thought.

Steve Teodecki, who had replaced an injured Mark DeRosa at quarterback and happens to be Chico's roommate, was joking the night before. Teodecki said if he ever got the chance, he would throw the ball to Chico no matter what. All this was going through his head. Chico set on the line of scrimmage instead of a yard back. Excitement had gotten the better of him, but junior receiver **Erik Thompson** backed him up to the right position. He regained his composure in time for the snap.

There he went, down the left side of the field, and curled toward the center. There was a linebacker defending him. As taught, he slid further inside. Teodecki fired the ball, and the catch was made just short of the end zone. "The 1st thing that went through my mind when he threw it was, 'God, don't drop it.'" Chico said. He jumped a little bit and caught the ball in his pads rather than with his hands. It was a catch nonetheless. He turned around and saw the goal line, and defenders coming at him from the sides. "I just kept thinking, 'I've got to get in,'" he said.

He dove and put the ball across the goal line. His knee came down on the 1-yard line. He looked up and was trying to find the referee to see the call. The referee hesitated, but then put his arms up. Chico rolled over, and everything was a blur. Teammates piled on top of him. "That was just a great thing to feel, knowing my whole team was behind me just for that one play," he said. The most memorable thing Mike Chico will take from the game was from friend and teammate Brian Higgins. "He had tears in his eyes. He was just so happy for me," Chico said.

1994: Awesome Again
After defeating Harvard in the above game, once again the Quakers faced Cornell having already clinched the Ivy title. The only thing on the line was another unbeaten season (and a 20-game winning streak). The only difference was that this year, the game was in Ithaca. Playing with a cast on the thumb of his throwing hand, and with the Quakers once again trailing by a 14-0 score, quarterback Mark DeRosa rallied the team to an 18-14 victory in the final minutes. A 54-yard TD pass from DeRosa to **Mark Fabish** and a 1-yard run by Terrance Stokes sealed the deal. The winning streak was now at 21.

Recollection from "The Man" Himself - Mike Chico, Class of 1995
My time at Penn was truly special, and the best memories that I have from those days involve the wonderful bonds and friendships that evolved from Penn football. I was a walk-on, converted high school quarterback-turned-receiver, and was hoping to make the travel squad my senior year. I had a really good summer of training; I came into camp in the best shape of my life and had a pretty decent camp. I just wanted to make a contribution on the field, on what was undoubtedly going to be a special team.
We were loaded at the skill positions, specifically receiver. Miles Macik would go on to shatter nearly every Penn receiving record and eventually earn a spot on the Detroit Lions. Mark Fabish was an electric returner and flanker. Leo Congeni was the same class as me, with great hands and route-running ability. Felix Rouse was a burner, a pure 4.3-40 guy who could stretch defenses. And Erik Thompson was a pure athlete. It was always hard to get on the field behind those guys But I think that is what made us so good at the position: We competed and challenged each other on the practice field, and once the game started, we were each other's biggest fans. We were a special group, on a special team, and I was truly fortunate to be part of it all.

As I said, my goal was to make the travel team, which consisted solely of receivers. For the Dartmouth game, which was up in Hanover, I was lucky enough to be the 6th receiver, the last guy on the bus. But then we had a bye and a couple of home games, and in that time, it was determined that my travel spot would best go to Billy Formosa, who was a defensive back by trade, but who was an absolute demon on special teams. He was a gunner on the punt team who caused all sorts of havoc on kickoff and kick return teams, too. It was clearly the right decision, because he needed to be on the field, and it was just unfortunate that it came at the expense of the 6th receiver slot. But such is life, and clearly we were a better team for him being there.

Fast forward to that Harvard game: in garbage time, I'm on the field, time is winding down and we were driving, but I didn't have opportunities on that drive to make a play. We kicked a field goal with only three minutes to go to put us up 26-0. On the ensuing kickoff, we force a turnover. And who forced that fumble? That's right: Billy Formosa. It was such poetry that he was the guy, the same guy who took my travel spot, that gave me the chance to be on the field for that one play. If he doesn't force that fumble, this isn't even a story. It's just amazing how it all comes together sometimes.

Luke Parker was the first person I met on campus freshman year, and we remain best friends to this day. Luke was also on the field for that play. He was a tight end and one of the open receivers on that play. He made a great chip block that helped keep a would-be tackler off me; and he was the 1st of my teammates to swarm me on the pile in the end zone. Kevin Lozinak (C '95, offensive lineman) is another close friend. It was he who walked up to the line judge after the play to ensure that they secured the football for me afterward. I still have that ball.

The play itself was just gravy on an otherwise tremendous season. As a football play, there wasn't much special to it: double-tight end set, twin receivers to the left, play-action pass with me running a curl route as the 1st read. The play action seemed to spring everyone open. I had a bit of an unfair advantage: Steve Teodecki, who was Mark DeRosa's backup at QB and in the game for that play, also happened to be a housemate of mine. The night before the game, Steve and I joked about the potential for "garbage time" in the Harvard game, and how he would change the play to throw me a ball if given the chance.

Every year on November 12 I email Steve just to say thanks for throwing me the ball, and he always replies: "Chico, there's no way I was throwing it to anyone but you." Anyway, before the snap, Erik backed me off the line, which was crucial: With double-tight ends, had I lined up on the line of scrimmage, I would have been covering an eligible receiver, and we would have been flagged for illegal formation. And maybe that play never happens, or, it gets called back afterward. Thank God for Erik. I ran my route, shuffled inside the LB, Steve put the ball on me and I just tried to get across the goal line.

But it is what followed that sticks with me the most: I'll never forget Luke being 1st on the pile. I'll never forget Kevin retrieving the ball. I'll never forget Brian Higgins, another house-mate, in tears on the sidelines. I'll never forget the pile-on in the end zone, all the great teammates and friends, celebrating the moment with me. It is better to see it on the video, because I can see some teammates coming off the sidelines to jump on.
Seeing Leo in particular always gets me. We were friends since freshman year, and always competing for the same spot on the field. I like to think we pushed each other and brought out the best in each other over those years, but maybe that's me just thinking wishfully. Leo was a great athlete on his own, but that's what you live for, especially as a walk-on: You want to contribute and be on the field, but there is so much desire to prove you belong on the field in the first place. Earning my teammates' respect mattered more to me than any one play or catch.

And that is really what I take away the most from that play. That is why the big pile-on is so special to me. Those are teammates and friends that I still keep in touch with. We had such love and respect for each other, and that comes through loud and clear in the celebration after that play. The best friends I have are the ones I met playing football at Penn. They shared that moment with me in 1994, and I've been lucky to share my life since Penn with them.

40. Changing of the Guard

November 4, 1995 - Princeton 22, Penn 9

"We've had a great run."

Tigers Dominate Quakers, Move toward Ivy Title

Penn coach Al Bagnoli was less than pleased when the refs disallowed an apparent touchdown in the 4th quarter of this 22-9 loss to Princeton. The TD would have brought Penn to within six points behind.

Until their defeat at Columbia earlier in this 1995 season, Penn had not lost a game since November 7, 1992. Between those two losses, Penn dominated its opposition, winning 24 consecutive games and claiming two straight undisputed Ivy League championships. In this much-anticipated game, however, almost exactly three years since that loss, things came full circle. 34,504 fans witnessed a changing of the guard atop the Ancient Eight, as the Tigers won 22-9, taking a huge step toward a league title of their own.

Princeton struck first like a lightning bolt, zapping the life out of the Quakers' homecoming crowd. Two touchdown passes by Tiger rotating quarterbacks put Penn in a 14-0 hole, with nine minutes still left in the 1st quarter. The Quakers' defense stiffened after that; however, the Penn offense could not take advantage, thanks to the tough Princeton defense.

Favorite target **Miles Macik** was constantly blanketed by a cornerback, safety and linebacker, and under the Princeton pass rush, quarterback **Mark DeRosa** could not find anyone else. Finally, in the 2nd quarter, the Quakers began to move the ball, aided by a couple of turnovers. First, an interception by strong safety **Nick Morris** set up a drive that resulted in a 32-yard field goal by **Jeremiah Greathouse**. Then, with 2:49 left in the 1st half, a botched snap gave Penn the ball at its own 47. Three runs and a reception by tailback **Jasen Scott** moved the ball to the Princeton 26. After a 5-yard scramble, DeRosa hit wideout **Felix Rouse** with two straight completions, the 2nd a 6-yard touchdown pass. A failed 2-point conversion left the score at 14-9 going into half-time. Momentum appeared to shift the Quakers' way.

But instead of hope, the 2nd-half kickoff brought disaster. The Quakers botched the return, forcing the offense to start from its own 3-yard line. After Penn gained only seven yards, a 10-yard punt into the wind gave the Tigers possession at the Quakers' 20. Then, on a key 3rd-and-8, Tiger QB Brock Harvey rolled right to escape pressure, and, just before reaching the sideline, zipped a pass to flanker Roly Acosta at the 2. A TD plunge over left tackle on the next play plus a 2-point conversion pushed the Princeton lead to 22-9.

The Quakers still had a chance to come back, but a long drive in the 3rd quarter ended when Princeton safety Jimmy Archie stepped in front of Macik and intercepted a DeRosa pass. Two consecutive opportunities deep in Tigers territory midway through the 4th period ended unsuccessfully on downs. The Princeton defense, which finished with five sacks, blitzed often and effectively, not allowing DeRosa time to complete his passes. After Penn's final attempt to score failed, the Tigers took over with 6:35 left in the game and ran out the clock. "We've had a great run," said Penn head coach Al Bagnoli.

Score by Quarters					
	1	2	3	4	Total
Princeton	14	0	8	0	**22**
Penn	0	9	0	0	**9**

Scoring Summary
Princeton -   Washington 15 pass from Harvey (Sierk kick)
Princeton -   Duffy 37 pass from Nakielny (Sierk kick)
Penn -   Greathouse 32 FG
Penn -   Rouse 6 pass from DeRosa (pass failed)
Princeton -   Washington 2 run (Godek pass from Harvey)
Attendance – 34,504

1995: Can't Win 'Em All
After this loss to Princeton, the Quakers easily won their final games against Harvard and Cornell. All that prevented the Quakers from attaining their 3rd straight Ivy title were an upset loss to Columbia earlier in the season, which stopped Penn's record win streak at 24, and a last-second, game-tying field goal by Princeton in *its* season finale vs Dartmouth. Although Penn didn't win it this year, the team had nothing to be ashamed of. The legacy of excellence they established – back-to-back unbeaten titles and 24 straight wins – will never be forgotten. Although Princeton won the 1995 Ivy title, this year's seniors will always be champions. As for the following season: hit by graduations, the 1996 team managed only a 5-5 record and a 5th-place finish in the Ivies.

41. Victory in the Gloamin'

November 8, 1997 - Penn 20, Princeton 17

"I did it a million times in practice and never came through that clean."

Penn Blocks Princeton FG, Then Greathouse Converts

*Placekicker **Jeremiah Greathouse** (4) beats Princeton with a 34-yard field goal with 0:08 left.*

As the sun set and a mist descended on Franklin Field, Penn's **John Bishop** heard the roar of the homecoming crowd when his left elbow deflected Alex Sierk's 46-yard, go-ahead field goal attempt with 2:38

left in the game. Nineteen yards downfield, on the Princeton 47-yard line, Bishop picked up the loose ball, giving the Quakers another chance to break a 17-17 tie in regulation. "I felt that this was the time," said Bishop, the team captain. "This was *my* season. I did it a million times in practice, and never came through that clean."

Quaker running back **Jim Finn** and the offensive line took over. With five straight rushes for 29 yards, Finn muscled Penn down to the Tigers' 17-yard line, setting up a 34-yard field goal with eight seconds remaining. After converting only seven of his previous 15 field goal attempts this season, Penn's **Jeremiah Greathouse** redeemed himself in front of 15,847 fans, giving Penn a 20-17 win over the Tigers and setting up a showdown in Cambridge with Ivy League leader Harvard. "I was in a good situation with a 17-17 tie," Greathouse said. "I couldn't lose the game. All I could do was win it. The guys on the field-goal blocking team did a great job. They were the ones that put me in that situation."

The game was a nail biter that never should have been. Penn held a 10-0 half-time edge. Greathouse opened the scoring with a 44-yard field goal in the 1st quarter, before Finn scored his 9th touchdown in four games early in the 2nd, on a 1-yard dive over the top. Down 17-3 with just over two minutes left in the 3rd quarter. Princeton's 2nd-string quarterback John Burnham, who came in due to an injury to starter Harry Nakielny, led the Tigers on three straight scoring drives. "He is a lot more of a scrambler," Penn coach Al Bagnoli said. "We were practicing more for the drop back game of Nakielny."

Allowing Burnham to complete passes across the field, the Quakers were surprised by the talent of the inexperienced quarterback. Penn's defense stood strong in the trenches, however, allowing only six net yards rushing in the game. In the Tigers' last series, after Burnham completed a 21-yard pass on 3rd-and-13, the Quakers' defensive line, led by **Doug Zinser**, stuffed Princeton running back Gerry Giurato for a 2-yard loss. On the next play, two fake handoffs did not fool Penn's **Mitch Marrow,** who tackled the Tigers quarterback on a rollout to the left. On 3rd-and-7, the Penn secondary forced Burnham to throw the ball away, so Princeton was forced to try Sierk's luck at the 46-yard field goal.

As for the Quakers' offense, its silent 4th quarter came after consistent play in the 1st 3, especially from Finn. The newly converted running back capped another big day with 146 yards on 33 attempts and a touchdown. In the middle of the 3rd quarter, Finn broke down the right side for a 57-yard gain. On that same drive, Penn quarterback **Matt Rader** used his athletic ability, carrying the ball into the end zone from five yards out, on a bootleg to the right side. Unfortunately, Rader, who was injured on the play, had to leave the game. Senior **Tom MacLeod** replaced Rader, but the offense went cold. With only one 1st down before the final drive of the game, the Quakers' offense gave Princeton time to come back. Although the Penn offense hit a lull, the team felt comfortable with the change at QB. "It did not affect our offense at all," Finn said. "We weren't worried."

Score by Quarters					
	1	2	3	4	Total
Princeton	0	0	6	11	17
Penn	3	7	7	3	20

Scoring Summary
Penn -   Greathouse 44 FG
Penn -   Finn 1 run (Greathouse kick)
Princeton -   Sierk 33 FG
Penn -   Rader 5 run (Greathouse kick)
Princeton -   Sierk 24 FG
Princeton -   Burnham 13 run (Giurato pass from Burnham)
Princeton -   Sierk 43 FG
Penn -   Greathouse 34 FG
Attendance – 15,847

*Defensive linemen **Adrian Puzio** (54) and **Mitch Marrow** (97) celebrate a fumble recovery by **Joe Piela** in the 1st quarter of the Quakers' 20-17 win over Princeton.*

1997: Forfeit

Per Ivy League rules, Penn's use of a player who was subsequently declared ineligible caused the Quakers to forfeit their five league victories in 1997, including the above game with Princeton. Thus, Penn's 6-4 overall season record became 1-9, and their 5-2 Ivy season record became 0-7. Bummer.

42. Champs Once Again

November 14, 1998 - Penn 41, Harvard 10

"They're Baack"

Penn 41, Harvard 10

*Wide receiver **David Rogers** (81) and teammates **B**ruce **Rossignol** (22) and **Adrian Puzio** (54) celebrate with the Franklin Field crowd, after Penn's 41-10 victory over Harvard clinched at least a tie for the Ivy league title.*

"Obviously, a complete role reversal from last year. They beat the hell out of us. and they deserved to win."
Tim Murphy, Harvard head coach

No disappointment. No let down. Not this time. One year after Harvard clinched the Ivy title after disposing of Penn by 33-0 in Cambridge, the Quakers turned the tables, defeating the visiting Crimson for their 1st Ivy League championship since 1994. "It's unbelievable," Penn linebacker **Darren MacDonald** said. "I was in tears with four minutes left to go in the game. It's the greatest feeling I have ever had." While Harvard showed little resemblance to last season's team, the Quakers did not even need the full 60 minutes to show their progress from last year. "Obviously, a complete role reversal from last year," Harvard coach Tim Murphy said. 'They beat the hell out of us, and they deserved to win."

Penn's offense needed only five plays from the line-of-scrimmage to take a 13-3 lead halfway through the 1st quarter. The Quakers' 1st possession began on Harvard's 31-yard line, after a 21-yard punt return by Penn's **Joe Piela**. Four plays later, Penn running back **Jim Finn** ran the ball into the end zone from eight yards out for his Ivy League-leading 14th touchdown of the season. "The guys up front on the punt return team did a great job. as they have been doing all year,'' Piela said. "It set the tempo. The offense got the ball, and they put it right in. That is how you want to start the game." On the 1st play of the Quakers' next possession, Penn quarterback **Matt Rader** found wide receiver **Brandon Carson** clear past Harvard defensive back Glenn Jackson for a 78-yard touchdown bomb. The Crimson's rushing defense, along with a few penalties, managed to slow Penn's offense for the rest of the half.

Midway through the 3rd quarter, Harvard backup quarterback Brad Wilford brought the Crimson to within 10 points, on a 2-yard touchdown pass to tight end Chris Eitzmann. But Penn then unleashed a potent passing attack to ignite the offense. After completing passes to Penn wide receivers **Jason Battung** and **David O'Neill,** Rader handed the ball to Finn, who scored from 16 yards out. "It seemed like Rader just hit every receiver with every pass," Harvard defensive tackle Brendan Bibro said. "They just took control of the game. It was anybody's game right there." Leading 27-10 with one quarter left, the Quakers added touchdowns by **Jason McGee** and Finn to increase the lead to 41-10, which was enough leeway for Penn fans to start chanting for the goal posts. With the win, the Quakers guaranteed themselves at least a tie for the Ivy title. While they were able to get pumped for Senior Day against Harvard, it would be potentially difficult for them to keep up their vigor for the following weekend, when they would travel to Ithaca.

Score by Quarters					
	1	2	3	4	Total
Harvard	3	0	7	0	**10**
Penn	13	7	7	14	**41**

Scoring Summary
Penn -   Finn 8 run (kick failed)
Harvard -   Giampaolo 32 FG
Penn -   Carson 78 pass from Rader (Feinberg kick)
Penn -   Battung 6 pass from Rader (Feinberg kick)
Harvard-   Eitzmann 2 pass from Wilford (Giampaolo kick)
Penn -   Finn 16 run (Feinberg kick)
Penn -   McGee 2 run (Feinberg kick)
Penn -   Finn 2 run (Feinberg kick)
Attendance – 14,909

1998: We're Back
The following week after the above victory, Penn soundly defeated Cornell in Ithaca, 35-21, to win the Ivy title outright again. The Quakers finished the season with an overall record of 8-2, and an Ivy League record of 6-1, with the only blemish being a 58-51 loss to Brown, in Providence. This time there were no forfeits. In the following year, despite the brilliant efforts of transfer quarterback **Gavin Hoffman**, Penn mustered only a 5-5 record. An overall winning record was thwarted by – surely you have it by now – a lackluster (20-12) loss to Cornell in the season finale at Franklin Field.

43. The Comeback

October 28, 2000 - Penn 41, Brown 38

"Never Say Die"

Down by 18 in 4th, Quakers Come Back to Win

Rob Milanese runs after one of his nine catches on the day; he caught the game-winning TD with 0:28 remaining, giving the Quakers a stunning 41-38 victory over Brown.

"I've never been a part of a game that meant so much and was so exciting at the end."
Gavin Hoffman, quarterback

In leading one of the most dramatic comebacks in the long and storied history of Penn football, **Gavin Hoffman** proved that he had the poise as well as the arm to be considered one of the Quakers' best-ever quarterbacks. With the Red and Blue trailing Brown 38-20 with only

5:04 to go, Hoffman took to the field on Penn's 39-yard line, having already thrown for 304 yards on the day. It was the 5th game this season in which he threw for over 300 yards. But it was touchdowns more than yardage that Penn needed now. And with time ticking away, it needed to score quickly.

"We just needed someone to step up and make a play, to get everyone back in the game," Hoffman said. That someone was Hoffman, who pinpointed Penn wide receiver **Rob Milanese** on a 48-yard bomb to put the Quakers on the Brown 8-yard line. Then an 8-yard touchdown pass to **Jason Battung** made the score 38-27.

Penn's defense held, and after a quick drive, Hoffman's 1-yard sneak into the end zone made the score 38-33, with 2:49 to go. Brown's coach inexplicably stuck to a passing attack, and the Bears couldn't move again. Starting on Penn's own 38 with 1:41 left, Hoffman led his team down the field again, and culminated the drive by hitting Milanese with a short swing pass on the Brown 7-yard line, which the junior receiver took into the end zone for a 39-38 Penn lead. After a successful 2-point conversion, another pass to Milanese, the comeback was complete.

Penn still had to deal with the Bears' potent offense one more time. Having allowed 24 points in Brown's previous five drives, the confidence of Penn fans was not high. But the enlivened Quaker defense stood strong, forcing the Bears to chuck a Hail Mary from the Brown 36-yard line on their final play. Bears' wide receiver Stephen Campbell, who led his team with 124 yards receiving, caught the ball in Penn territory. Just before being tackled, the all-time Ivy League receptions leader lateralled the ball to a teammate.

Next came four more Brown laterals. "I ran straight for the goal line," said Penn cornerback **Joey Alofaituli** about this desperation play by Brown. "Regardless of what was going to happen, they just couldn't score. I was scared out of my mind. They had five laterals, and my heart was beating faster with each one." The Bears' final lateral, though, went over the fingertips of its intended receiver, sending the ball out of bounds with no time left. Alofaituli's fear then turned to jubilation as he realized the Quakers had finally won the wild game. "Just to see that ball finally drop to the floor with the time gone out was amazing," he said. After watching the ball roll across the sideline, Alofaituli's teammates and coaches stormed Franklin Field to celebrate the sensational win, which kept Penn in a 4-way tie for 1st place in the Ivy League, with just three games remaining. Hoffman, the catalyst of the miraculous comeback, had 476 yards passing, shattering his previous Penn record of 399. Hoffman also had ended eight yards short of **Reds Bagnell**'s 50-year-old mark of 490 yards total offense in a game.

Score by Quarters					
	1	2	3	4	Total
Brown	14	0	14	10	**38**
Penn	13	7	0	21	**41**

Scoring Summary
Penn   -   O'Neill 19 pass from Hoffman (kick failed)
Brown -   Buchanan 39 pass from Webber (Jensen kick)
Penn   -   Verille 5 run (Feinberg kick)
Brown -   Ferguson 5 interception return (Jensen kick)
Penn   -   Ryan 15 run (Feinberg kick)
Brown -   Webber 1 run (Jensen kick)
Brown -   Campbell 7 pass from Webber (Jensen kick)
Brown -   Campbell 15 pass from Webber (Jensen kick)
Brown -   Jensen 22 FG
Penn   -   Battung 8 pass from Hoffman (Feinberg kick)
Penn   -   Hoffman 1 run (run failed)
Penn   -   Milanese 7 pass from Hoffman (Milanese pass from Hoffman)
Attendance – 13,208

Recollection from Gavin Hoffman, Class of 2002
We were anxious and excited going into the game. Brown had beaten us the previous three years, all high-scoring games. It was going to be a challenge, but we were starting to play well and felt we could beat

them. The 1st half of the game went as expected, the teams matching each other score for score.

However, we came out flat after half-time, our offense stalled while Brown scored a couple touchdowns to start to pull away. Midway through the 4th quarter, we were down 18 points. The sideline energy was gone, and fans had already started leaving. I don't recall which specific play triggered it, but the momentum sharply and suddenly turned in our favor. The defense quickly shut them down for several 3-and-outs, Joe Phillips and our special teams had two long punt returns, and our receivers Colin Smith, Jason Battung, Doug O'Neil and Rob Milanese each made big catches for quick scoring drives. Brown helped us by continuing to throw the ball late into the game while the whole team played nearly perfect football over the final five minutes, outscoring them 21-0 to win in the closing seconds. That comeback was the turning point in our season. We won each of our remaining games, including several other comebacks, and finished the season as Ivy League champions.

44. The Comeback, Part Deux

November 11, 2000 - Penn 36, Harvard 35

"Kicking is far from a strength. We tried to not have to do that today."

Quakers Top Crimson in Another Nail-biter

Gavin Hoffman *(2) had another red-letter day, throwing for 394 yards and two touchdowns.*

As Harvard kicker Robbie Wright's wobbly 33-yard field goal attempt sailed wide left with 10 seconds left on the clock, the Penn football team rushed the field, jubilantly releasing a season's worth of tension. The Quakers had just stolen their 3rd consecutive come-from-behind victory by the narrowest of margins, escaping with a 36-35 win, which kept them squarely in control of their own destiny in their quest for the Ivy League title. Penn's dramatic triumph over Harvard meant that the Quakers remained in a 1st-place tie with Cornell, whose own comeback win (over Columbia) set up a final week showdown for the Ivy championship in Ithaca.

Junior quarterback **Gavin Hoffman** continued his assault on the Penn passing record books, leading an offense that for most of the afternoon was as crisp as the cold November wind. Already the most prolific passer in Quaker history heading into Saturday's contest, Hoffman completed 34 of 47 pass attempts for 394 yards and two touchdowns, including the game-winner to **Rob Milanese** with 1:24 left. Hoffman spread the ball to nine different receivers, finding tight end **Ben Zagorski** 10 times for 125 yards and a touchdown and Milanese eight times for 84 yards, capped off by the 16-yard game-clincher. Running back **Kris Ryan** added 74 yards rushing and a touchdown on 25 carries.

The game got off to a rollicking start. A 1-yard sneak by Hoffman put the Quakers up 7-0. But on Harvard's 1st play from scrimmage, Carl Morris tied the game at 7-7, taking junior quarterback Neil Rose's short pass 77 yards for a touchdown. Just two minutes later, the Crimson took a 14-7 lead on Ben Butler's 54-yard interception return. Penn appeared to have righted its ship when lineman **Kevin Martin** forced a Rose fumble, and cornerback **Fred Plaza** pounced on the loose ball at the Harvard 16. Three plays later, Hoffman threw his 1st touchdown pass of the day – a 13-yard strike to Zagorski. The momentum then swung clearly back to the Quakers' side, when they opened the 2nd quarter with a 9-play, 72-yard scoring drive, which put them back on top by 21-14.

The Crimson then broke *another* big play, again checking Penn's steady offensive surge. Tailback Nick Palazzo burst through the line of scrimmage and a host of would-be Penn tacklers for a 66-yard touchdown scamper, tying the score at 21. Penn kicker **Jason Feinberg** chipped in an 18-yard field goal to put the Quakers up by a score of 24-21 lead at the half, but this lead did not feel comfortable -despite controlling the ball for more than 23 minutes and scoring 24 points in the 1st half, Penn led by only 3, and Harvard had scored all 21 of *its* 1st-half points in less than one minute, collectively.

Then, in the 3rd quarter the Penn offense flagged, scoring only a field goal by Feinberg. Harvard started *its* 2nd and 3rd drives with fumbles on 1st down, but Penn went 3-and-out after the 1st fumble recovery, and Feinberg missed a 44-yard field goal into a 17 mile-per-hour headwind.

Imbued with new life, Rose drove Harvard 73 yards, completing a 1-yard touchdown pass to Chris Stakich for a 28-27 lead. After freshman linebacker Dante Balestracci returned a Hoffman interception to the Penn 29-yard line, Rose found Morris for another touchdown, increasing the Crimson's lead to 35-27. But Penn's defense stifled the Crimson in the 4th quarter, taking advantage of costly Harvard penalties and allowing only one 3rd-down conversion on five attempts. Another Feinberg field goal made the score 35-30. After a Crimson punt with 1:36 left in the game, Penn took the ball at the Harvard 48-yard line. Hoffman wasted no time conjuring up memories of comebacks past, first completing a 32-yard pass to **Jason Battung** and then finding Milanese for a 36-35 lead.

The 2-point conversion failed, leaving Harvard a window to spoil the Quakers' homecoming with even a field goal. And it almost happened. Rose drove his team 69 yards to the Penn 11-yard line with 54 seconds to go. But a false start and three incomplete passes left the Crimson with a 4th-and-15 with 15 seconds left, forcing Harvard coach Tim Murphy to send out freshman kicker Wright for a 33-yarder into the wind. Wide left. Jubilation for Penn.

"Kicking is far from a strength," said Murphy, whose kickers had converted just three of 12 field-goal attempts this season. "We tried to not have to do that today." But after Wright's attempt missed badly and Hoffman took a knee to run out the clock, Penn players and fans breathed a sigh of relief, with students spilling out of the stands onto the Franklin Field turf toward the newly fortified west goal posts. It's just as well the goal posts refused to come down, because only a Penn victory at Cornell on the following Saturday would win Ivy laurels for the Quakers.

Score by Quarters					
	1	2	3	4	Total
Harvard	14	7	14	0	35
Penn	14	10	3	9	36

Scoring Summary
Penn - Hoffman 1 (Feinberg kick)
Harvard - Morris 77 pass from Rose (Wright kick)
Harvard - Butler 54 interception return (Wright kick)
Penn - Zagorski 13 pass from Hoffman (Feinberg kick)
Penn - Ryan 1 run (Feinberg kick)
Harvard - Palazzo 66 run (Wright kick)
Penn - Feinberg 18 FG
Penn - Feinberg 23 FG
Harvard - Stakich 1 pass from Rose (Wright kick)
Harvard - Morris 26 pass from Rose (Wright kick)
Penn - Feinberg 21 FG
Penn - Milanese 16 pass from Hoffman (pass failed)
Attendance – 18,715

2000: Cardiac Kids
After the above game against Harvard, Penn fans needed no further medications for heartburn or panic attacks. In the season finale against Cornell in Ithaca, the Quakers walloped the Big Red, 45-15, to clinch yet another outright Ivy title. Penn's only Ivy loss in 2000 came at the hands of Yale, 27-24, in New Haven. In 2001, only a 28-21 loss to Harvard in Cambridge prevented another perfect season and Ivy championship. But there was always next year.

Franklin Field Saturdays

45. "GameDay"

November 16, 2002 - Penn 44, Harvard 9

"I founded Penn – this is MY school. Of course I'm picking them to win!"

"Prime Time" Quakers Crush Crimson

Franklin Field hosted another 1st, as ESPN's marquee college sports show – College Game Day – visited a Football Championship Subdivision (FCS) school for the 1st time. In the show's biggest segment, former coach and now analyst Lee Corso dressed up as Penn founder Ben Franklin to make his customary picks. He correctly chose the Quakers, of course, as the Red and Blue steamrolled Harvard en route to a perfect 7-0 Ivy League record and another championship. Said Ben, "I founded Penn – this is MY school. Of course I'm picking them to win!"

Some Penn fans may have been concerned that the pre-game hoopla of ESPN *Gameday* would distract their team, but they needn't have worried. The players had been waiting for this game since the previous year's 28-21 loss to Harvard, which had ruined their title hopes. Despite the cold, steady rain and the raucous atmosphere, nothing was going to cause them to lose their focus on winning this game. The 18,630 spectators knew from the kickoff that Penn was totally locked in.

On Harvard's opening drive, linebacker **Steve Lhotak** recovered a fumble by Harvard quarterback Neil Rose at the Crimson 12-yard line, which set up a 27-yard field goal by **Peter Veldman**. When Penn quarterback **Mike Mitchell** was sacked in the end zone for a safety, Harvard players celebrated, and it appeared that the game might be a contest after all. However, after receiving the free kick, the Crimson's drive ended quickly. At midfield, **Vince Alexander** hit Rose on a safety blitz, forcing a fumble, which bounced right into the hands of defensive end **Chris Pennington,** who waltzed into the end zone.

Harvard didn't know it yet, but the game was essentially over at that point, as the Quakers scored on their next four consecutive possessions in the 1st half, and the rout was on: After another Veldman field goal, Mitchell threw an 18-yard touchdown pass to **Stephen Faulk**, a 12-yard pass to **Dan Castles** and a 33-yarder to **Erik Bolinder**. Half-time score: Penn 34, Harvard 2.

Mitchell threw one more TD pass: a 22-yarder in the 3rd quarter to **Rob Milanese.** "Rob is unbelievable," said Mitchell. "He just goes and gets the ball." **Roman Galas** completed the scoring for Penn with a 41-yard field goal. Finally, with under five minutes left, Harvard scored their only touchdown of the day, albeit against the Penn reserves.

With the victory, Penn clinched at least a share of the Ivy championship and set up a chance to achieve an undefeated league season – and sole possession of the title – in the next and final game at Cornell. "It was very special, so emotional," Mitchell said. "Everything is going through your head. It's the best feeling. And to have our fans in Franklin Field share it with us made it that much better."

Score by Quarters					
	1	2	3	4	Total
Harvard	2	0	0	7	9
Penn	13	21	7	3	**44**

Scoring Summary
Penn -   Veldman 27 FG
Harvard -   Safety, Mitchell tackled in end zone
Penn -   Pennington 51 fumble return (Veldman kick)
Penn -   Veldman 23 FG
Penn -   Faulk 18 pass from Mitchell (Veldman kick)
Penn -   Castles 12 pass from Mitchell (Veldman kick)
Penn -   Bolinder 33 pass from Mitchell (Veldman kick)
Penn -   Milanese 22 pass from Mitchell (Veldman kick)
Penn -   Galas 41 FG
Harvard -   Fratto 9 pass from Fitzpatrick (Blewett kick)
Attendance – 18,630

2002: Domination

With another outright Ivy League championship already in hand, Penn shut out Cornell in Ithaca, 31-0, to complete an undefeated Ivy League season. The powerful Quakers finished with an overall record of 9-1, losing only at Villanova, 17-3.

Recollection from Mike Mitchell, Class of 2004

This was probably the biggest game I've ever played in and certainly one of the most important games of which I've been a part.

I recall the beginning of the season when we were taking team photos, and word got out that the 2002 Penn Quakers were picked to finish 4th in the league in the pre-season poll. Granted, we lost a lot of talented players to graduation. We had a lot of talent on the 2002 team – but nobody outside of the program knew it. Yet.

The week before our game versus Harvard, we pounded Princeton pretty good at their place. We were taking cold showers after the game – somehow Princeton's hot water was not working – when our director of football operations, James Urban (current QB coach of the Baltimore Ravens) walked in and said, "Gentlemen, get ready for next week. ESPN's College Game Day is coming to Franklin Field for our game versus Harvard." The whole locker room went nuts. We celebrated that night only, and then it was all business during the week. No FCS program had yet hosted ESPN College Game Day, and the Penn Quakers would be the 1st.

We had been in some big games during the year, including knocking off Number four Lehigh and ending their 26-game regular-season winning streak. We also played a tough game at Villanova, in which they won and handed us our only loss of the season. Villanova went on to the play in the semi-final game of the 1-AA championship. The Penn versus Harvard game for the last several years had determined the eventual Ivy League Champion. This was a big game.

The entire week was full of excitement as camera crews were present. Coaches Bagnoli and Coen did their best to keep our normal routines. Our team practiced hard. We knew we were going to show the entire country how hard Penn played and how good this Ivy League team was. I recall coming out of the tunnel with my teammates and seeing the crowd and hearing them cheer for us as we entered- Franklin Field.

It must have been about the time Lee Corso put on his Ben Franklin outfit, predicting a win for the Quakers, that the fans went bonkers It was almost as if I was in a dream for this brief moment and the lights were coming on for a grand performance on a grand stage and everyone was cheering. It was an incredible feeling of energy and adrenaline. As we-settled in on the sideline and prepared for kickoff, I recall thinking, "Wow, our stadium is packed on our side. I wonder what it would have been like if it weren't 35 degrees and raining. This whole stadium might be full."

OK. Focus. Back to the task at hand. Our offense started off slowly. I missed a read and got sacked in the end zone for a safety. It took us some time to get in a rhythm as Harvard's defensive game plan was always good. Their schemes were good and their players were good. Thank God for our defensive players, who were the backbone of our team that year. They were constantly forcing turnovers and making big plays and big stops. I believe that defense averaged giving up something like 50 yards rushing per game. It was an insane statistic that would be difficult to break: less than 15 yards-rushing per quarter for the year. Wow. Harvard quarterback Neil Rose was a good player. The headlines called him the Michael Vick of the Ivy League. Michael Vick was an amazing player who transformed the game. Our defense hit Neil Rose so hard, they knocked him out of the game. The backup quarterback for Harvard was none other than Ryan Fitzpatrick, who is still playing for the Miami Dolphins. Harvard also had All-American receiver Carl Morris, who was a 2-time Ivy League player of the year. Our defense held him to three catches for 20 yards.

The game changed when Chris Pennington picked up a fumble about midfield and returned it for a touchdown. When Chris got to the end zone, he turned around, faced the crowd, lifted the ball and pretended it was a beer mug and he was drinking it. It was the coolest celebration I've seen and a foreshadow of what was to come. It was the turning point in the game.

Our offense came alive and reeled off four touchdowns in short order. First a screen pass to the speedy Stephen Faulk, who followed his blockers and high-tailed it into the end zone. Next Danny Castles out-jumped Harvard's secondary in the back of the end zone and somehow managed to get both feet down. Then Erik Bolinder caught a deep post off a play-action for a touchdown. And finally, Rob Milanese easily juked his defender to get wide open for a touchdown. Milanese's touchdown celebration was pretty good, too. He went up to the goal post like he was going to dunk it and then did a finger roll. Classic.

The offensive line played as fantastic a game as they had done all year. Matt Dukes, Michael Powers, Chris Kupchik, Dylan D'Ascendis, Ben Noll and Chris Clark were incredible players, and I am forever grateful to each one of them.

Once the game was over, the crowd left and the lights went off, it was a moment to reflect on our accomplishment. The Penn football Class of 2004 team never lost a game at Franklin Field. That is a legacy we are proud of. It may never happen again. This team started the conversation and provided a good argument for why the Ivy League Champion should be allowed to compete in the NCAA playoffs.

46. All's Well That Ends Well

October 25, 2003 - Penn 34, Yale 31 (OT)

"The feeling is relief."

Quakers Survive Eli Comeback, Win in Overtime

*Penn wide receiver **Matt Makovsky**, whose catch deep in the red zone helped set up a 2nd-quarter field goal for the Quakers.*

On this Franklin Field Saturday, the Quakers avoided what would have been an embarrassing and bitter loss to the Yale Bulldogs, when **Peter Veldman**'s 23-yard field goal in overtime sent the Penn fans home at least relieved, if not ecstatic. With his team trailing by 21 points with 11 minutes remaining in the game, Yale quarterback Alvin Cowan led the Bulldogs to three unanswered touchdowns with his precision passing, wiping out the Penn lead and tying the score. However the Red and Blue rallied for the victory, when **Casey Edgar** blocked a field goal attempt in overtime that would have given the Bulldogs the lead, and then Veldman made the winner.

Behind the punishing running of sophomore back **Sam Mathews** and the brilliant passing of quarterback **Mike Mitchell**, Penn led by 17-3 at half-time, and appeared to be in complete control. After an 18-yard TD run by Mathews in the 3rd quarter and a 22-yard touchdown pass from Mitchell to **Dan Castles** in the 4th, the Penn lead looked insurmountable at 31-10. However, somebody forgot to tell the Yale team. three touchdown passes by Cowan tied the score at 31-31, the 3rd one coming with 32 seconds remaining in regulation. Penn still almost managed to win without overtime: three Mitchell pass completions gave Veldman a chance to win it, but his (career-longest) 45-yard attempt was short and wide.

In overtime, Yale got the ball 1st, but had to settle for a field goal attempt, which Edgar foiled. Penn had the ball, and Mathews tore through the Yale line for 15 yards on the 1st play, taking the ball all the way to the Yale 10. On 3rd down, Veldman split the uprights, and the game was over. "The feeling is relief," said Al Bagnoli. Penn, unbeaten in 2003, had won its 20th in its last 21 Ivy League games. three weeks later, the still-undefeated Quakers traveled to Harvard and defeated the Crimson 32-24, to clinch the Ivy championship.

Score by Quarters						
	1	2	3	4	OT	Total
Yale	0	3	0	28	0	31
Penn	7	10	7	7	3	34

Scoring Summary
Penn – DeSmedt 1 run (Veldman kick)
Yale – Troost 41 FG
Penn – Barr 11 pass from Mitchell (Veldman kick)
Penn – Veldman 18 FG
Penn – Mathews 18 run (Veldman kick)
Yale – Cowan 5 run (Troost kick)
Penn – Castles 22 pass from Mitchell (Veldman kick)
Yale – Henley 13 pass from Cowan (Troost kick)
Yale – Plumb 17 pass from Cowan (Troost kick)
Yale – Plumb 13 pass from Cowan (Troost kick)
Penn – Veldman 23 FG
Attendance – 16,510

47. Castles in the Air

November 22, 2003 - Penn 59, Cornell 7

"Records are made to be broken."

Quakers Annihilate Big Red, Finish at 10-0

Penn wide receiver **Dan Castles** *(18) catches a pass in the previous week's game versus Harvard. In this game vs Cornell, Castles finished with four touchdown receptions, a new Penn record.*

"Even though we'd already won the title, we still came out like we had something to play for. You want to go out with a bang."
Mike Mitchell, Penn quarterback.

The Quakers quickly dispelled any fan worries about their team suffering an emotional letdown for this game. They scored a touchdown on their 1st play from scrimmage and never looked back - three more touchdowns followed on their next three drives, all in the 1st quarter. Before Cornell knew what hit them, it was 28-0 Penn. Shattering offensive records everywhere, the Quakers cruised to a 59-

7 victory before 8,203 spectators, to complete their 1st undefeated season (10-0) since 1994.

The 1st Penn touchdown came on a 60-yard pass from quarterback **Mike Mitchell** to wide receiver **Dan Castles**. Next came a 1-yard TD run by **Sam Mathews**, a 3-yard TD pass to tight end **Brian Adams** and another TD pass (of 23 yards) to Castles. Castles finished with nine catches, for 204 yards and four touchdowns. The yardage figure was the 4th best for receivers in Penn history. The four receiving touchdowns were a new Penn record. Mitchell's totals were 22 for 30, for 371 yards and five touchdowns (also a new Penn mark). Finally, the 59 points scored and the 52-point margin of victory were Penn's largest since joining the Ivy League.

"I can't give our seniors and our whole football team enough credit," said head coach Al Bagnoli. Another Ivy League championship and undefeated season were in the books.

Score by Quarters					
	1	2	3	4	Total
Cornell	0	0	7	0	7
Penn	28	7	10	14	59

Scoring Summary

Penn –	Castles 60 pass from Mitchell (Veldman kick)
Penn –	Mathews 1 run (Veldman kick)
Penn –	Adams 3 pass from Mitchell (Veldman kick)
Penn –	Castles 23 pass from Mitchell (Veldman kick)
Penn –	Castles 12 pass from Mitchell (Veldman kick)
Penn –	Veldman 35 FG
Cornell –	Kellner 20 pass from Busch (Weitsman kick)
Penn –	Castles 6 pass from Mitchell (Veldman kick)
Penn –	Perskie 4 run (Veldman kick)
Penn –	Ambrogi 4 run (Veldman kick)

Attendance – 8,203

2003: Total Domination

Another year, another undefeated (10-0) season, and another outright Ivy League title. This Penn senior class won its last 16 straight games overall (the 2nd longest streak in the nation) - 15 straight in the Ivy League, and 24 out of its last 25. Penn's seniors were winners in all 19 games they played at Franklin Field, and in 26 of their 28 Ivy games – the best four-year mark for a Penn team ever. This senior group also came away with three league titles, this one by a full three games. This 2003 season was also a pinnacle for Penn football for a while. Beset by injuries to some key players, some personal tragedies, and some just plain bad luck (especially in the kicking game), the Quakers would not win another Ivy League title for another six years.

Recollections from Jake Perskie, Class of 2004

When the game was over, and we'd smoked our cigars, we grabbed the cup, commandeered a Penn facilities golf-cart (itself a story) and headed up to Smokey Joe's. That's us in the picture. I have the eye-black on, Pat McManus is Number 4, and Kevin Stefanski is Number 30, holding the cup. We took a lot of pictures that night (including one of my Mom drinking from the cup), and many of our families took pictures with us in our pads holding the cup. But this picture is my favorite.

By the fall of 2003, things had settled into a rhythm. Pat McManus, Kevin Stefanski, and I were seniors and had survived another Al Bagnoli training camp. Although we no longer lived together –we'd been housemates until that summer when Kevin's long-time girlfriend (and now, wife) made him move out of our Superfund site on Baltimore Avenue into more respectable housing – we still spent Thursday nights together, working the door and stocking the bar at Smokey Joe's.

On Thursdays, as we waited for hordes of our soon-to-be drunk classmates to pack the bar, we'd shoot the sh**, trash-talk each other – junior fullback Kevin DeSmedt, a world-class trash-talker in his own right, worked with us too – and look at the pictures on the wall. One picture near our perch at the door was a group of football guys at the bar in their pads. It was old enough that the uniforms and equipment looked alien to us, probably from the late 1980s or early 1990s. Someone, I forget who, mentioned one night that if we went undefeated and won the Ivy League title, we should bring the Class of 1925 Trophy to the bar.

As the weeks went on and we racked up wins, the idea began to crystalize. We were playing Cornell, at home, under the lights, for the last game of our careers. You know what happened on the field that night. A law-school friend who had played linebacker on that Cornell team once confided in me that their plan at the half was to try to keep us from scoring 100 points.

We took a lot of pictures that night, but the one above is my favorite. Paul Ryan (owner of "Smokey Joe's," in the white shirt) likes to say that it's what you do in the bar, not on the field, that gets your picture on the wall. Sure, we won on the field, but that picture captures one of my favorite memories of my football career, and it's a story that began and ended in the bar.

48. The Fumble

October 30, 2004 - Penn 20, Brown 16

"It hurts to get the ball to the 1-yard line and not take it in."

Fallon Forces Fumble, Quakers Beat Bears

Dan Castles *scores Penn's 2nd touchdown of the day to give the Quakers their 1st lead, 13-10.*

Penn led Brown for only three minutes in this game, but a fumble recovery by senior defensive end **Bobby Fallon** at Penn's 1-yard line and a 9-play, 88-yard scoring drive gave the Quakers a 20-16 victory over the Bears at Franklin Field. **Sam Mathews** scored the decisive touchdown with just 50 seconds remaining, giving the junior two touchdowns on the day.

A game that saw both teams combine for 15 punts turned on a defensive play deep in Red and Blue territory. With Brown leading 16-13 with three minutes left in the 3rd quarter and poised to add to its lead, Fallon stripped the Bears' running back Nick Hartigan before the latter could cross the goal line and recovered the ball himself, to give Penn possession and new life.

The turnover did not prove immediately beneficial, because the teams exchanged possession an astonishing seven times before Penn began a 4th quarter drive that ensured its 19th-straight Ivy League victory. After a 10-play Brown drive stalled, their punter pinned Penn at its own 12-yard line. Penn quarterback **Pat McDermott** then came alive, hitting six of eight passes to three different receivers. All six completions gained 12 or more yards and enabled the Quakers to move the ball down the field quickly. **Matt Carre** caught four of those passes, and soon Penn was on Brown's 2-yard line. A defensive pass-interference call in the end zone gave the Red and Blue a new set of downs, and one play later Mathews bulldozed over the goal line from two yards out, putting Penn ahead by 20-16, with under one minute left on the clock. The Bears' final drive ended with Penn's **Bryan Arguello** intercepting a pass in the end zone.

The game was tight all the way. Brown jumped on the board quickly, scoring on a 30-yard touchdown pass on the game's opening drive. Penn immediately answered with an 8-play, 64-yard drive of its own, which concluded when Mathews punched it in from two yards out to pull the Quakers within 1, 7-6. A Brown field goal ended the 1st quarter scoring at 10-6. In the 2nd quarter, **Dan Castles** scored Penn's 2nd touchdown of the day – the 26th of his career, tying **Miles Macik** as Penn's all-time leader – to give the Quakers the lead at 13-10, with five minutes remaining in the half. Brown responded with another field goal, and the teams went to the locker room tied at 13.

Early in the 3rd quarter, the Bears went ahead by 16-13 on another field goal. Then, with a little more than three minutes left, they drove to Penn's 2-yard line, largely on the sledgehammer running by Hartigan. But those last two yards came down to a matter of a 220-pound irresistible force (Hartigan) meeting a 230-pound immovable object

(Fallon). The immovable object won. Fallon refused to get out of Hartigan's way, forced him to fumble, and recovered the ball at the 1. No one knew it yet, but Bobby Fallon had saved the day for Penn.

Score by Quarters					
	1	2	3	4	Total
Brown	10	3	3	0	16
Penn	6	7	0	7	20

Scoring Summary
Brown –   Schreck 30 pass from Vita (Morgan kick)
Penn –   Mathews 2 run (kick failed)
Brown –   Morgan 40 FG
Penn –   Castles 9 pass from McDermott (Zoch kick)
Brown –   Morgan 31 FG
Brown –   Morgan 35 FG
Penn –   Mathews 2 run (Zoch kick)
Attendance – 12,314

2004: 2nd Best

Two weeks after the above Brown game, Penn and Harvard, both undefeated in the Ivies, faced off for the championship at Franklin Field. It was not Penn's day. Freshman quarterback **Bryan Walker** made his collegiate debut in place of the injured Pat McDermott and performed exceptionally well, but it wasn't enough. Harvard held the Red and Blue offense in check for most of the afternoon, as senior punter **Josh Appell** recorded a season-high eight punts. Harvard, on the other hand, jumped out to a 14-3 lead in the 1st half and never looked back, ultimately cruising to a 31-10 victory. Penn defeated Cornell, 20-14, in the season finale at Ithaca, but Harvard beat Yale in *its* finale, so it was only 2nd place for the Quakers this year, albeit a solid 2nd.

Recollection from Bobby Fallon, Class of 2005

It was Halloween-eve 2004. Mischief Night has been a trickster's tradition in Philadelphia since the late 1700's, and the day's football game built on the legend. The tension on campus was already palpable because the following Tuesday was Election Day. Two Yalies, George W. Bush and John Kerry, were battling for the Oval Office – another American tradition.

Aside from the presidency, the next biggest Ivy battle was between the back-to-back Ivy champion Quakers and an upstart Brown team. Led by Nick Hartigan, the Bears had a bruising offense and strategized to play keep-away through long drives and clock-devouring possessions. We knew what to expect. In the previous season Hartigan led the NCAA in yards per game, and it was fashionable at the time to entrust one running back with 30 touches. After all, this was the pro-era of Marshall Faulk and Brian Westbrook. The press hyped Hartigan, especially because he was a finalist for a Rhodes Scholarship. Although he never received the scholarship, he settled at Harvard Law. Aim for the stars, so to speak.

Above all things in this game, I remember his devastating fumble best. As a defensive end from South Florida, I took a lot of pride in two things: not losing edge containment and showboating if the mood struck. This play gave me the opportunity for both.

It was 3rd down and goal from the 1-yard line. They had Hartigan, and it didn't take a Rhodes finalist to know they were going to run it. We had nine men in the box. The play was driving toward Weightman Hall, and Brown ran an outside zone sweep in the direction of the south stands. The offensive tackle tried to reach-block me, but I was able to meet him with force and keep my outside arm free. Hartigan took the handoff and reluctantly looked inside.

There he saw our All-World defensive tackle Michael Sangobowale shedding a double team, and Hartigan wisely tried to bounce outside. Sprinting at an angle, I was able to get an arm around him, and our hard-hitting future-pro cornerback Duvol Thompson finished the job with a big collision. The3 of us tangled up at the 1-yard line. Just as the whistle blew, I saw the ball on the turf. I grabbed the rock, jumped to my feet and triumphantly held the ball high in one hand toward our home stands. I had no idea if it was a fumble or not, but I was committed to celebrating it. I have always thought that enthusiasm is contagious, and perhaps, in that moment, the roar of the crowd swayed the referee to call a fumble.

Our offense took over from the one and put together a signature 99-yard winning touchdown drive, with Sam Mathews scooting past future New York Giant Zak DeOssie into the endzone. A dejected Hartigan was next to me at the press conference after the game. "I thought I was down," he said "But you never are supposed to let the ref make a call."

It was my senior class's final win at Franklin Field, the last of the winningest class in Ivy history. To this day I have followed Hartigan's career. He is now a federal prosecutor in Georgia. Perhaps he felt such injustice that he has dedicated his life to righting wrongs, or maybe he's just another lawman who couldn't handle Mischief Night in Philadelphia.

49. Déjà vu All Over Again

October 20, 2007 - Yale 26, Penn 20 (3 OT)

"It's déjà vu all over again."

Quakers Fall to Yale in Triple Overtime

Yale successfully defends a Penn pass in the end zone, in overtime.

Oh, no. Not again. Penn lost a football game in overtime to Yale for the 2nd year in a row, this time in *triple* overtime. And once again, this loss was not without controversy.

Controversy # 1 -- Did Yale running back Mike McLeod get into the end zone on 3rd down during Yale's possession in the 3rd overtime? It appeared that he bounced off the ground about a half-yard shy of the end zone, but his momentum – and reach – put the ball over the line. However it appeared, the refs quickly signaled a touchdown.

Controversy # 2 – In that same overtime, facing 4th-and-goal from inside the one and needing a touchdown to tie the game, Penn rolled a halfback pitch to the left. **Joe Sandberg** caught the pitch and quickly realized he had nowhere to go. Yale had sniffed out the play. Sandberg turned back, came to the right side, and with several more Yale defenders bearing down on him, had the wherewithal to throw a pass to fullback **Nick Cisler** in the end zone. Touchdown. Hold on – a flag fluttered. Penalty against Penn for an ineligible man downfield. The ball was brought back five yards and the 4th down replayed. This time, quarterback **Bryan Walker** tried to hit **Braden Lepisto** on a slant route, but the ball sailed a bit and slid through the leaping Lepisto's outstretched hands. Final score: Yale 26, Penn 20.

The above final sequence capped off a wild affair at Franklin Field, providing several riveting moments for the homecoming crowd of 15,668 and a national television audience. It was another hard-to-swallow defeat for Penn – starting with the previous year's game at Yale, the Quakers had now played and lost four overtime games.

Yale had dominated its opponents in this 2007 season, and for a quarter Saturday it looked like the Bulldogs would add the Quakers to their list. After a Bryan Walker pass was intercepted at the Penn 46-yard line, Mike McLeod broke through up the middle and raced into the end zone, making the score 7-0 for Yale. But Penn's defense stiffened, and in the 2nd quarter the Quakers took seven plays to get to the 9-yard line, then scored when Sandberg surprised everyone with a halfback option pass to **Josh Koontz**, and a 7-7 tie at half-time.

The teams managed only to trade field goals in the 2nd half, as both defenses stiffened. A 31-yard field goal by Yale tied the game at 10-10 in the final quarter, but both teams had little success moving the ball for the rest of regulation, and when Penn's **Tyson Maugle** picked off an attempted long bomb by Yale QB Matt Polhemus in the final seconds, the stage was set for overtime. Yale started 1st, and, advancing to the 2-yard line, did not mess around, going to McLeod for a touchdown. Yale 17, Penn 10. Penn's 1st possession was a little more adventurous, helped by a pass interference penalty on 4th-and-5, on the next series Walker found **Marcus Lawrence** for a TD reception. Yale 17, Penn 17.

During the 2nd overtime, Penn went 1st, and facing 4th down, opted for a field goal. **Andrew Samson** was good on his 23-yard attempt to give Penn a 20-17 lead. Yale got to Penn's 7-yard line, but on 4th down also opted for the tie, and barely got it when a bad snap was well-handled by the Bulldogs holder, and the kick split the uprights. Tie again: Yale 20, Penn 20.

Onto the 3rd overtime. Yale again went 1st, again went for the quick strike and, thanks to a facemask penalty, scored a touchdown on McLeod's run. Per NCAA rules, Yale was forced to go for two points. They failed in that attempt, but it only set the stage for the Quakers' unsuccessful final gasp, as described above.

Score by Quarters						
	1	2	3	4	OT	Total
Yale	7	0	0	3	16	**26**
Penn	0	7	0	3	10	**20**

Scoring Summary
Yale - McLeod 46 run (Kimball kick)
Penn – Koontz 9 pass from Sandberg (Samson kick)
Penn – Samson 43 FG
Yale – Kimball 31 FG
Yale – McLeod 2 run (Kimball kick)
Penn – Lawrence 5 pass from Walker (Samson kick)
Penn – Samson 23 FG
Yale – Kimball 21 FG
Yale – McLeod 1 run (pass failed)
Attendance – 15,668

2007: A Tough Year
One never likes to blame the officials, but, rightly or wrongly, some strange rulings by the zebras -including in the above Yale game - right from the opener, helped doom the Quakers to their 1st losing season (4-6) under Al Bagnoli. However, a 45-9 rout of Cornell in the season finale at Franklin Field gave rise to hope for the following season. Although they did not earn the championship in 2008 either, the visible improvement rightly brought forth anticipation for 2009.

50. Home Cooking on Homecoming

November 7, 2009 – Penn 42, Princeton 7

"There's no place like home."

Quakers Stew Tigers on Homecoming Day

Brian Levine *(32) tackles Princeton's Akil Sharp during the Quakers' rout of the Tigers.*

In front of an energetic homecoming crowd of 14,027, the Quakers didn't disappoint. They dominated their archrival Princeton, 42-7, scoring Penn's largest victory over the Tigers since 1943. Senior quarterback **Kyle Olson** threw for a career-high three touchdown passes, junior fullback **Luke DeLuca** had a career-high two rushing touchdowns, and senior defensive back **Chris Wynn** had his 1st career interception return for a touchdown, as the Quakers won their 6th straight game to improve to 5-0 in Ivy play. This win set up a showdown of Ivy unbeatens the following week, when Penn would travel to play Harvard with the Ivy title on the line.

It didn't take long for Penn's offense to put points on the board. After stopping Princeton on its 1st possession, Olson completed back-to-back passes to senior **Kyle Derham** and DeLuca, for 21 and 29 yards, respectively. The longest reception in DeLuca's career set up his 1-yard touchdown run on the next play, for a 7-0 lead three minutes into the game. The score remained 7-0 until Princeton mishandled Penn's punt to start the 2nd quarter, and senior linebacker **Jake Lewko** recovered the fumble. Two plays later, junior wideout **Matt Tuten** caught Olson's pass in the middle of the field near the 5-yard line and raced straight into the end zone. 14-0 Penn.

Jonathan Moore's interception on Princeton's next drive set up the Quakers' next touchdown. Starting from the Princeton 35, Olson immediately connected with Derham for 27 yards to set up 1st-and-goal, and on 4th-and-goal from the 1, with the crowd on its feet, DeLuca rushed for his 2nd touchdown. 21-0. Princeton got on the board on their ensuing possession, closing out the scoring in the 1st half at 21-7 – as close as Princeton ever got.

Penn scored on its opening possession in the 2nd half, going 66 yards on six plays in just over three minutes. Olson capped off the drive with a pass in the flat to Derham, who ran seven yards down the sideline for a 28-7 edge. Two Princeton punts later, Penn put together its longest drive of the season, marching 84 yards for a commanding 35-7 advantage. From the 3-yard line, Olson faked a sneak and nearly tripped, before lobbing a pass into the middle of the end zone to tight end **Luke Nawrocki**. In the 4th quarter, Penn's defense got in on the scoring, as Wynn intercepted Princeton QB Tommy Wornham's pass and returned it 60 yards for a touchdown, leaping into the end zone with 11:01 remaining in the game, putting the Quakers up by 42-7 and closing out the scoring on the day.

"We're headed in the right direction," said Al Bagnoli.

Score by Quarters

	1	2	3	4	Total
Princeton	0	7	0	0	7
Penn	7	14	14	7	42

Scoring Summary

Penn –	DeLuca 1 run (Samson kick)
Penn –	Tuten 14 pass from Olson (Samson kick)
Penn –	DeLuca 1 run (Samson kick)
Princeton –	Kerr 2 pass from Wornham (Bologna kick)
Penn –	Derham 7 pass from Olson (Samson kick)
Penn –	Nawrocki 3 pass from Olson (Samson kick)
Penn –	Wynn 60 interception return (Samson kick)

Attendance – 14,027

51. "We're Baack"

November 21, 2009 – Penn 34, Cornell 0

"Offense Sells Tickets; defense wins championships."

Quakers Shut out Big Red, Clinch Title Outright

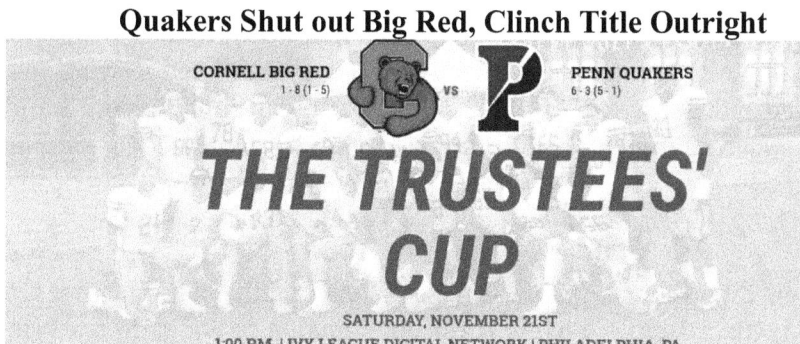

"We have broad expectations here."
Al Bagnoli, Penn head coach

Outright Ivy League champions. The Penn football team left no doubt as to which was the best team in the Ivy League in 2009, dismantling Cornell by 34-0 at Franklin Field. In front of 9,018, the Quakers clinched the program's Ivy League record 11th outright championship and 14th overall. In the 116th meeting between the two Ivy rivals, the Quakers also claimed ownership of the Trustees' Cup from Cornell for the 3rd straight year.

There was no better way for the Quakers defensive unit to finish the season. They claimed their second shutout - the first time a Penn team had done that since 2002 - and held Cornell to just four first downs and 110 total yards (61 of those yards came on Cornell's final drive, with Penn's starting unit out of the game.

It wasn't just the defense that put forth a stellar performance - Penn was dominant in all phases of the game, and it was the Quakers' special teams that made the 1st move. With 10:41 remaining in the first quarter, linebacker **Erik Rask** blocked Drew Alston's punt and recovered it on the 3-yard line. On the next play, running back **Lyle Marsh** rushed for a 3-yard touchdown to put Penn up 7-0. On Penn's next possession, **Bradford Blackmon**'s 26-yard rush set up a 23-yard field goal by **Andrew Samson**. After another Cornell punt, the Quakers started at the Big Red 45-yard line. It took just four plays to set up junior quarterback **Keiffer Garton**'s 1st rushing touchdown of the season. The 8-yard run put the Quakers up 17-0 with just 1:51 to go in the half, but the Quakers weren't done. The defense forced a quick 3-and-out, giving the offense the ball 33 seconds later at their own 33-yard line. The Red and Blue executed the 2-minute drill to near perfection. Senior **Kyle Olson** completed four straight passes, reaching just inside the Cornell 30-yard line. With seven seconds left, Samson tacked on a career long 46-yard field goal, to give Penn a 20-0 half-time lead.

On their 1st possession of the 2nd half, Penn ran the ball nine times, as Garton, Blackmon and **Matt Hamscher** totaled 54 yards to reach the Big Red 9-yard line. On the only pass play of the drive, Garton connected with **Luke Nawrocki** in the end zone, making the score 27-0. After a terrific goal-line stand, which ended with a sack by **Brian Wing**, Penn marched down the field yet again. After six straight running plays, Garton threw to **Kyle Derham,** floating a perfectly placed pass that hit the senior captain in stride in the end zone. That closed out the scoring at 34-0, with 1:51 remaining in the 3rd quarter. In the 4th quarter, Cornell made one final attempt to break the shut out; however. with just over one minute remaining, the Quakers stuffed a rush attempt near the goal line, ensuring the shutout.

Score by Quarters					
	1	2	3	4	Total
Cornell	0	0	0	0	**0**
Penn	10	10	14	0	**34**

Scoring Summary
Penn – Marsh 3 run (Samson kick)
Penn – Samson 23 FG
Penn – Garton 8 run (Samson kick)
Penn - Samson 45 FG
Penn – Nawrocki 9 run (Samson kick)
Penn – Derham 25 pass from Garton (Samson kick)
Attendance – 9,018

2009: Champs Again..
Head coach Al Bagnoli admitted that "We have broad expectations here," and that going six years without a title was "too long." The motto that defense wins championships rang true this season, as the outstanding play of the defense, led by **Jake Lewko** and **Chris Wynn,** helped deliver the 14th Ivy League football title to Penn. This season was the 7th outright championship for head coach Al Bagnoli, more than any other coach in league history. This was also Bagnoli's 5th unbeaten Ivy coaching season, more than any other program had ever achieved.

52. Introducing "Billy Ball"

October 2, 2010 - Penn 35, Dartmouth 28 (OT)

"When you're the champion, this is how people are going to play you."

QB Ragone Sneaks Quakers Past Big Green

*Quarterback **Billy Ragone** (10) hands off to **Brandon Colavita** (33), against Dartmouth.*

Facing second-and-goal from the Dartmouth 1-yard line in overtime, sophomore quarterback **Billy Ragone** called his own number, sneaking in for his 4th touchdown (3 rushing, one passing) of the day. In this thrilling Ivy opener. Ragone's keeper gave Penn a 35-28 lead. The defense then slammed the door on the Big Green, forcing three incompletions, including a failed 4th-and-4 pass that lineman **Drew Goldsmith** knocked down. The win, before a crowd of 10,407, was the Quakers' 9th straight over an Ivy opponent and their 12th win in their last 13 meetings with the Big Green.

The Quakers scored on their 1st drive, which Ragone finished with a 14-yard scamper into the end zone. Dartmouth answered right away with a drive of its own, that culminated in a 5-yard touchdown run to tie the score. But Penn again went right down the field, scoring on another rushing touchdown by Ragone, this one from six yards, and recaptured the lead. two minutes into the 2nd quarter, Dartmouth again responded, on a 12-yard touchdown pass from quarterback Connor Kempe to John Gallagher. Penn went back up with another sustained drive, this time with **Ryan Becker** under center. The freshman connected on four of five passes to get the Quakers down to the Dartmouth 4-yard line. From there, running back **Brandon Colavita** bulled into the end zone, giving Penn a 21-14 lead at the half.

Penn started with the ball in the 2nd half and marched down the field again. Going 4-for-5, Ragone led a drive that burned seven and a half minutes off the clock. Four Quakers (**Jeff Jack, Luke DeLuca, Bradford Blackmon** and Ragone) ran the ball, and on 3rd-and-goal from the 2, Ragone rolled right and threw to an open DeLuca for a touchdown and a 28-14 lead.

Penn now appeared to have the game in hand, but that was a mirage. A Dartmouth interception set up the Big Green at the Penn 20-yard line, altering the momentum of the game. four plays later, the Big Green faked a field goal and converted a 1st down to set up 1st-and-goal from the 4-yard line. They scored on the next play, when Kempe again connected with Gallagher in the end zone. Penn still led, 28-21 with 3:46 left in the 3rd quarter, but that lead didn't last long. On their next possession, just before the quarter ended, Dartmouth went 75 yards for a TD in just five plays.

With the game tied, each team had a chance to win in the closing minutes, but both failed to capitalize, leading to overtime and Ragone's heroics. Speaking of heroes, defensive lineman **Brandon Copeland** led the team with nine tackles, and linebacker **Zach Heller** had 8, of which two resulted in a loss of yardage.

"When you're the champion, this is how people are going to play you," said Penn head coach Al Bagnoli.

A new Ivy season had begun, and "Billy Ball" had arrived with it.

Score by Quarters						
	1	2	3	4	OT	Total
Dartmouth	7	7	14	0	0	28
Penn	14	7	7	0	7	35

Scoring Summary
Penn –   Ragone 14 run (Samson kick)
Dartmouth –   Schwieger 1 run (Schmidt kick)
Penn –   Ragone 6 run (Samson kick)
Dartmouth –   Gallagher 12 pass from Kempe (Schmidt kick)
Penn –   Colavita 4 run (Samson kick)
Penn –   DeLuca 3 pass from Ragone (Samson kick)
Dartmouth –   Gallagher 4 pass from Kempe (Schmidt kick)
Dartmouth –   Reilly 10 pass from Kempe (Schmidt kick)
Penn –   Ragone 1 run (Samson kick)
Attendance – 10,407

53. Another Championship

November 13, 2010 - Penn 34, Harvard 14

"I think it's really, really hard to win back-to-back titles. It speaks volumes..."

Ivy Champs Again

***Aaron Bailey** (87) celebrates as **Billy Ragone** (10) scores on a 6-yard run, putting the Quakers up by 27-0 over Harvard.*

After a slow start, the Penn team became unstoppable, earning an impressive 34-14 win over Harvard. Thus the Quakers clinched a share of its 15th Ivy League title, their 8th under head coach Bagnoli. The team had a chance to win the title outright for the 2nd year in a row, if it won at Cornell on the following Saturday.

The defenses dominated the 1st quarter. The Quakers drove deep into Harvard territory on their 1st drive, but Harvard stopped them on the

4th down at the 28-yard line. Harvard recovered a fumbled punt by Penn near midfield, but nothing came of that, either.

In the 2nd quarter, however, a Penn punt hit a Harvard blocker inside the Crimson's 10-yard line, and Quakers recovered it at the 9. Although Penn was unable to punch it in, **Andrew Samson** nailed a 19-yard field goal, and Penn was up 3-0, with 12:22 to play. Harvard attempted to tie with 5:35 left, but **Erik Rask** blocked the 39-yard field-goal attempt. Penn immediately made the Crimson pay, driving 61 yards for the score as **Brandon Colavita** ended the drive with a 3-yard TD run, putting the Quakers up by 10-0.

Early in the 3rd quarter, **Bradford Blackmon** turned a near disaster into a big play: a Harvard punt bounced deep in Penn's territory, and in the process of keeping it out of the end zone, a Crimson player knocked it back in play. Blackmon was able to beat a Harvard player to the ball just at the line, scooped it up and raced along the right sideline nearly to the Penn 39. Colavita then knocked off a big gain, starting a 6-play Penn drive all the way to a touchdown. The score came when quarterback **Billy Ragone** found **Jeff Jack** on a short pass, and Jack found all kinds of room to run it in from 25 yards out, increasing the lead to 17-0. Penn's defense made the next big play, when **Justyn Williams** tipped a Harvard pass into the hands of **Daniel Ritt,** who returned it to the Crimson 45. A few plays later, Samson knocked home a 45-yard field goal, and the Quakers were up by 20-0.

Even though more than five minutes remained in the 3rd quarter, Harvard clearly understood the situation they were in – going for it on a 4th down in their own territory. The pass play was incomplete however, and the Quakers took over at the Crimson 38-yard line, taking seven plays to reach the end zone. Ragone did the honors this time, following his blockers through the right side for a 6-yard score that made it 27-0. Harvard finally got on the board with 11:04 left in regulation, to make the score 27-7, but after an attempted onside kick failed, Penn got the ball at the Crimson 38. Just two plays later, Colavita raced untouched around left end for a 35-yard score that put the Quakers' lead back up to 27. Harvard eventually added a late touchdown, but Penn's 33 seniors had finished their careers at Franklin Field with *another* Ivy championship.

"I think it's really, really hard to win back-to-back titles. It speaks volumes of your team's work ethic, character and focus," said Al Bagnoli.

Score by Quarters	1	2	3	4	Total
Harvard	0	0	0	14	14
Penn	0	10	17	7	34

Scoring Summary
Penn –   Samson 19 FG
Penn –   Colavita 2 run (Samson kick)
Penn –   Jack 25 pass from Ragone (Samson kick)
Penn –   Samson 45 FG
Penn –   Ragone 6 run (Samson kick)
Harvard –   Cook 31 pass from Winters (Mothander kick)
Penn –   Colavita 35 run (Samson kick)
Harvard –   Gordon 3 run (Mothander kick)
Attendance – 12,546

2010: And Again
Penn did go on to clinch the Ivy title outright with a convincing 31-7 victory over Cornell, in Ithaca. The following season proved less kind to the Quakers, however, as a 37-20 loss to Harvard in Cambridge ended their chances for a repeat, and a season-ending loss to Cornell at Franklin Field left them in a tie for 2nd place.

54. Great Scott

October 13, 2012 - Penn 24, Columbia 20

"Beam us up, Scotty."

Lopano Punts Help Push Penn past Lions

*Penn kicker **Scott Lopano** gets off one of his great punts, which were one of the keys to victory.*

In the previous season, **Billy Ragone** broke a 20-20 tie at Columbia's Kraft Field with a 7-yard game-winning touchdown run with 25 seconds left. This year, Penn had to climb an even steeper hill. The Lions went up by 10 with 10:57 remaining, on a 31-yard touchdown run by Marcorous Garrett – his 2nd of the day. But Ragone led a hurry-up offense 86 yards in just 3:30 to pull within 20-17, with 7:27 to play.

The drive nearly stalled at the Columbia 35-yard line, before Ragone found **Lyle Marsh** for 16 yards to convert on a 4th-and-7. Two plays later, Ragone sailed a pass up the seam, over the Lions' defense and into the hands of tight end **Mitchell King** for a 16-yard touchdown – the 1st catch of King's collegiate career. After a pair of punts, the Lions started from their own 6-yard line with 4:09 to go. But the defense forced another punt, and the Quakers took over at their own 38 with just 2:26 and one timeout remaining.

On 3rd-and-9 from the Columbia 41, Ragone connected with Marsh again, this time for 23 yards down to the Columbia 18-yard line. **Jeff Jack** rushed for seven yards, and Ragone hit Marsh for five more, setting up a 1st-and-goal at the Columbia 6, with a minute left. Two plays later, Ragone scrambled to his left and lofted a pass to the back corner of the end zone. Marsh was there for the catch, and the Quakers led 24-20. "It was a broken play," said Ragone, who engineered his 6th career 4th-quarter or overtime comeback. "I broke the pocket, and Lyle kind of slipped to the back of the end zone, and I threw it up to him, and he came down with it for a big play for us."

But Columbia wasn't done. Starting from their own 25, they marched down to the Penn 19 with 12 seconds left, then took two shots at the end zone. The 1st pass fell incomplete. On the final play of the game, the Penn defense pressured Columbia QB Sean Brackett, who threw across the field, where his receiver, Hamilton Garner, caught the ball at the 2-yard line. The only Penn player in the area was **Dan Wilk**, who wrapped Garner up as the time expired, saving the win for the Quakers and allowing the crowd to breathe again.

The 1st half was not a precursor to the drama of the 2nd half, as the teams combined for 10 punts and just nine points on three field goals, with Columbia taking a 6-3 lead into the locker room at half-time. Penn regained the lead on the 1st possession of the 2nd half, on a 13-yard TD pass from Ragone to wideout **Conner Scott**. Columbia went up 13-10, on Garrett's 1st touchdown run of the game at the 6:05 mark of the 3rd quarter. The Lions nearly struck again on their next possession, but senior captain **Brandon Copeland** blocked a 47-yard field-goal attempt just three plays into the 4th quarter. A short while later, though,

Garrett's touchdown gave the Lions the 20-10 lead and set the stage for the Quakers' wild comeback.

Spotlight: Senior punter **Scott Lopano** starred on special teams, matching a career high with nine punts and averaging 45.4 yards per punt. He had a long punt of 60 yards, pinning three inside the Columbia 20-yard line. Lopano also moved into 3rd-place all-time at Penn, with 165 career punts, one short of **Ryan Lazzeri** (1998-2001) for 2nd place. One could argue that he was the star of this game, in which he also coincidentally graced the cover of the game program.

Score by Quarters					
	1	**2**	**3**	**4**	**Total**
Columbia	0	6	7	7	**20**
Penn	0	3	7	14	**24**

Scoring Summary
Penn –   Loftus 37 FG
Columbia –   Eddy 40 FG
Columbia –   Eddy 38 FG
Penn –   Scott 13 pass from Ragone (Loftus kick)
Columbia –   Garrett 15 pass from Brackett (Eddy kick)
Columbia -   Garrett 31 run (Eddy kick)
Penn –   King 16 pass from Ragone (Loftus kick)
Penn –   Marsh 6 pass from Ragone (Loftus kick)
Attendance – 6,189

55. Sweet Sixteenth

November 10, 2012 – Penn 30, Harvard 21

"R-E-S-P-E-C-T – Find out what it means to me"

Quakers Down Crimson for Share of Ivy Crown

*Defensive tackle **Brandon Copeland** (52) sacks Harvard quarterback Colton Chapple in the end zone for a safety, clinching the victory for the Quakers.*

> "It just meant so much for him (**Billy Ragone**) to come back out of the locker room and be on the field with us."
> **Lyle Marsh**, running back

Just as the pre-season projections had indicated, this game had championship implications. The winner would earn a share of the Ivy crown. The teams kicked off just after noon on national television, and for three hours they engaged in a battle that lived up to the level of their respective championship programs. Penn won the day, waiting until the final seconds to wrap up a 30-21 decision. The game made viewers realize that they were watching something special, regardless of how it turned out. Both teams played hard-nosed football, and there was no discernible trash talk. At the end, the players met at midfield and shook hands, congratulating each other on jobs well done and showing the respect that these teams have for each other. Penn or Harvard had now won the championship each of the last five years, and 10 of the 12 in the 21st century to date.

Outside of the Penn locker room, one would have had a hard time finding anyone who would have made the Quakers the favorite in this particular contest. But the Red and Blue wasted no time in declaring themselves, taking the opening kickoff and needing just 2:45 to drive 69 yards for a touchdown. The scoring play was a beauty, as quarterback **Billy Ragone** fooled the Harvard defense into believing he was going underneath with a pass but instead went over the top to a wide-open **Conner Scott** for a 32-yard touchdown.

On Penn's next possession however, Harvard intercepted a Ragone pass near midfield. Six plays later, Harvard QB Colton Chapple ran it in from four yards out, tying the score at 7-7. Thanks in large part to a 47-yard run by **Lyle Marsh,** Penn responded quickly, going 81 yards in 10 plays. They found paydirt when Ragone ran for three yards just inside the right pylon for a 14-7 lead. In the 2nd quarter, Harvard tied things up again, but Penn used a sustained drive to go in front a 3rd time. The Quakers went up 21-14 when Ragone, who had a pair of nice runs on the drive, found a wide-open **Ryan O'Malley** on the left side of the end zone. That ended the 1st half scoring.

The teams went scoreless in the 3rd quarter, which unfortunately ended with Ragone leaving the game with a serious ankle injury. He returned, not to the field, but to the sideline – still seated, pads on, in the cart that drove him off. It backed up to the sideline so he could watch the game. It was a poignant moment that brought the Quakers' emotions to a high boil, if they weren't there already. "It just meant so much for him to come back out of the locker room and be on the field with us," said Lyle Marsh.

Enter senior **Andrew Holland**, who already had had more than his share of reps in this season. Picking up where Ragone left off, Holland handed off twice to Marsh, then lofted a beautiful 18-yard pass into the end zone that sophomore tight end **Mitchell King** wrested away from a Harvard defender to make the score 28-14. This appeared to wake up Harvard. Hurrying down the field, the Crimson drove to their 3rd touchdown of the day. With 10:42 left, Penn got the ball back, with its lead back to a single possession at 28-21. For the next six minutes, neither team gained a 1st down.

Then, on its 3rd drive with Holland at the helm, Penn finally broke through. Marsh ran for seven of his career-high 130 yards, then five more to gain a big 1st down near midfield. With the clock now inside of three minutes and the field tilted in their favor, the Quakers ran three straight times, forcing the Crimson to use all three timeouts. Finally **Scott Lopano** punted, and Harvard took a fair catch at its 11-yard line, with 1:38 to play. (Note: Lopano was once again an unsung hero, as six of his eight punts pinned the 3rd-highest scoring offense in the FCS inside the 20-yard line).

Harvard fans were now hoping for a miracle score. They got a score, all right, but no miracle. On 1st down, sophomore linebacker **Dan Davis** sacked Chapple for a 1-yard loss. On 2nd down, sophomore defensive end **Feerooz Yacoobi** made another sack, this time for seven yards. On 3rd down came the dagger. Chapple never stood a chance against the Quakers' withering rush. Perhaps poetically, it was Penn's 2012 captain, **Brandon Copeland**, who wrapped Chapple up in the end zone for the safety that delivered a 16th Ivy League championship to the Quakers - their 3rd in the last four years, and the 9th for head coach Al Bagnoli.

But one more game remained. Penn was off to Cornell to face a Big Red squad that dropped 48 points on them a year ago, in a 10-point Cornell win at Franklin Field. The outright title was hardly going to be a "gimme."

Score by Quarters					
	1	2	3	4	Total
Harvard	7	7	0	7	21
Penn	14	7	0	9	30

Scoring Summary
Penn –   Scott 32 pass from Ragone (Loftus kick)
Harvard –   Chapple 4 run (Mothander kick)
Penn –   Ragone 3 run (Loftus kick)
Harvard –   Scales 1 run (Mothander kick)
Penn –   O'Malley 2 pass from Ragone (Loftus kick)
Penn –   King 18 pass from Holland (Loftus kick)
Harvard –   Juszczyk 1 pass from Chapple (Mothander kick)
Penn –   Copeland - safety – tackled Chapple in end zone
Attendance – 8,910

2012: Fooling the Prognosticators
In a tense, tight affair in Ithaca in the finale, decided only in the final play, Penn prevailed over Cornell, 35-28, winning another outright championship. The members of this Penn senior class joined the Classes of 1985, 1986, 1987 and 2004 in earning three championship rings during their careers. After a lackluster loss to Yale in New Haven earlier in the season, the team could have packed it in. But, per captain Brandon Copeland, "We stayed together and got closer. This season is a testament to, 'As long as you believe, anything is possible.'"

Recollection from Brandon Copeland, Class of 2013
"What I remember most about this game is that we had come together as a team. After a somewhat listless loss to Yale in New Haven, we defeated Brown and Princeton in close games. Now we were facing a good Harvard team at Franklin Field, and we needed a victory to clinch at least a share of the Ivy title.

Harvard was a heavy favorite on this day, but we were locked in and focused from the get-go. We scored on our 1st drive when our quarterback, Billy Ragone, hit Conner Scott with a touchdown pass. Harvard was not used to playing from behind, and they appeared stunned. They did come back to tie the score, but the message had been sent, and we quickly scored again to make it 14-7. Harvard tied it up again, but we scored right before the half ended to make it 21-14. In the locker room, Coach Bagnoli was pretty calm, basically telling us to keep doing what we were doing.

Ironically, I think the turning point of the game was when Billy Ragone went down late in the 3rd quarter with a serious leg injury. We wanted to win the game for our leader, so it fired us up when he returned to cheer us on from the sideline, on a cart. Andrew Holland replaced Billy, and we had great confidence in him as well, as he was experienced and had a great arm. Andrew quickly threw a touchdown pass, which put us up 28-14. Harvard scored a touchdown with about 10 minutes left to make the score 28-21, then had the ball with one last chance to score, starting at around their own 10-yard line with under two minutes to play. After we pushed them back to their 3, on 3rd down I put a move on their offensive lineman and sacked the Harvard QB in the end zone for a safety, which sealed the victory for us. We erupted in joy after that.

One of my best memories of the game is that my family was in attendance and got to witness the game and its great finish, in which I had a hand."

56. Last Man Standing

October 5, 2013 - Penn 37, Dartmouth 31 (4 OT)

"At first, I was thinking 'What the heck are you doing?' But once he got the edge..."

"Marathon Men" Outlast Big Green

David Park *(54, center) blocks the potential game-winning field goal as time expires in regulation.*

And on and on it went, until...

When Penn kicked off to Dartmouth to start this game at Franklin Field, junior **Kyle Wilcox** was nowhere to be found among the running backs on Penn's depth chart. Three hours and 49 minutes later -- after the Quakers and the Big Green had played 60 minutes of regulation football, three full overtimes, and one possession of a 4th -- it was

Wilcox who dramatically ended things. With Penn facing a 3rd-and-5 at the Dartmouth 20-yard line and needing just a field goal to win this marathon, Wilcox took a handoff from quarterback **Billy Ragone,** bounced around the right side, stiff-armed a Big Green defender, and beat the rest of them to the sideline. The next thing you know, he was in the end zone, and Penn had escaped with a 37-31 victory. Ragone was expecting Wilcox to simply drive straight ahead to set up a field goal attempt. But Wilcox had other ideas. Said Ragone, "At first, I was thinking 'What the heck are you (Wilcox) doing?' But once he got the edge…I was just happy to get a win."

Thus ended *the longest game in Ivy League history*, one that featured blocked field goals, fumbles returned for touchdowns, and back-and-forth action that left fans on both sides completely drained.

In this Ivy opener for both teams, Wilcox had the winner, but the biggest hero of the day was senior linebacker **David Park**. He was all over the place for the Quakers, with two of the biggest plays of the game coming via his hands. In the 2nd quarter, he gave Penn a 14-7 lead with an 84-yard fumble recovery for a touchdown. While that play was huge, the one he made at the end of regulation was gigantic. With just four seconds left in regulation and the game tied at 21-21, Dartmouth lined up for the game-winning 21-yard field goal. However, Park again stepped up, blocking Riley Lyons' chip shot and stunningly sending the game to overtime.

Penn had the 1st possession in overtime, and drove all the way to the 5-yard line. However, on 4th-and-1, the Quakers opted to go for it and were stuffed at the line of scrimmage. Dartmouth suddenly had the game in its hands again. But Penn forced a 4th down and Lyons -- maybe still thinking about his kick in regulation -- hooked his 34-yard attempt wide left, to give the Quakers new life once again. Dartmouth started the 2nd OT with the ball, and needed just three plays to hit paydirt. Led by Billy Ragone, the Quakers responded. On a day when he became just the 2nd player in Penn history to go over 6,000 career yards in total offense, it was Ragone who got Penn to the 3rd overtime. Facing 3rd-and-12 at the 27-yard line, he escaped a collapsing pocket and found daylight along the Penn sideline, where he rumbled all the way to the end zone.

That tied the score at 28-28, and sent the game into a 3rd overtime. Penn started with the ball, and after three plays the Quakers put their faith in junior **Connor Loftus**. He rewarded them with a 38-yard field goal that went right between the uprights. On their next series, Dartmouth went nowhere, and the game was back again on the foot of Lyons. This time he delivered, knocking home a 40-yard field goal to knot the game at 31-31. Dartmouth started the 4th OT with the ball, and appeared to have scored a touchdown on a pass play; however, the Big Green was called for a personal foul, which nullified the TD. After that, Dartmouth got no closer than the 20-yard line, and on 4th down Lyons attempted a 42-yard field goal. Wide left, again. That set the stage for Wilcox's heroics, and a truly wild Penn victory celebration.

Score by Quarters						
	1	2	3	4	OT	Total
Dartmouth	7	0	7	7	10	31
Penn	7	7	7	0	16	37

Scoring Summary
Dartmouth – Pierre 1 run (Lyons kick)
Penn – Taylor 4 pass from Ragone (Loftus kick)
Penn – Park 84 fumble recovery (Loftus kick)
Dartmouth – Bakes 11 pass from Williams (Lyons kick)
Penn – Elespuru 3 run (Loftus kick)
Dartmouth – Williams 2 run (Lyons kick)
Dartmouth – Schoenthaler 12 pass from Williams (Lyons kick)
Penn – Ragone 27 run (Lyons kick)
Penn – Loftus 38 FG
Dartmouth – Lyons 40 FG
Penn – Wilcox 20 run
Attendance – 12,017

57. Missing the Point

November 23, 2013 – Cornell 42, Penn 41

"Let the kid play today, coach – I've got a headache."

Furious Quaker Rally Misses the (Extra) Point

Cornell's Tre Minor (99) blocks Penn's extra point attempt, which would have tied the game at 42.

"We were looking for a spark."
Al Bagnoli, Penn head coach, on his decision go to freshman QB Alek Torgersen.

In its 2013 season finale against Cornell, after watching the Big Red build a big lead, Penn mounted a furious rally, which was blocked at the most inopportune time. In the 120th meeting between these programs, Penn lost 42-41, with the 83 combined points being the second-most in the history of the series. Cornell also claimed the Trustees Cup from the Quakers for the 2nd time in the last three years. With leads of 14-0 and 21-7 in the 1st half, the Quakers seemed set to cruise to victory. Instead, they were staring up at a 21-point deficit with

7:49 to play, trailing the Big Red by 42-21. Enter freshman quarterback **Alek Torgersen**, who led a brilliant comeback attempt.

First, Torgersen connected with sophomore wideout **Cameron Countryman** from 45-yards out with 7:09 to play, on a strike which was the 1st career touchdown for both players. After Penn's defense put up a stop, Torgersen again went to the air for a Penn score, connecting with senior **Ty Taylor** on a 25-yard touchdown pass, bringing the score to 42-35 with 2:52 to play. Then the defense dialed up a turnover at just the right moment – senior **Sam Chwarzynski** stepped into a Cornell screen pass on 3rd-and-18, and returned the pick 39 yards for a touchdown, bringing Penn to within 1, pending the extra point. However, Cornell's Tre Minor blocked the point-after attempt, denying Penn the tie. Cornell received the ensuing kickoff and ran out the clock.

On Senior Day, 5th-year quarterback **Ryan Becker** had helped stake Penn to a 21-7 lead midway through the 2nd quarter, throwing a career-high three touchdown passes along the way. But those points were Penn's last for the next 30 minutes of play, as Cornell mounted a rally behind Jeff Matthews, their star quarterback, scoring 35 unanswered points in the process. Matthews had a hand in four of the five touchdowns, throwing for three and running in a 1-yard sneak of his own, to help the Big Red build a 42-21 lead. The lone non-Matthews touchdown came off a blocked punt that the Big Red recovered in the end zone.

Spotlight: Billy Ragone

Due to injury, 5th-year quarterback **Billy Ragone** was extremely limited in action, but he participated in the game's first two plays. He capped his career with a six-yard pass to **Ryan Mitchell,** giving the receiver the milestone of at least one catch in 25 straight games. Ragone had one of the greatest careers in school history. In addition to a school record 56 total touchdowns, Ragone finished his career as Penn's 2nd-most productive offensive player ever (behind **Gavin Hoffman**), with 6,724 total yards. Ragone also finished 3rd all-time at Penn in career passing yards, career completions and career passing touchdowns.

Score by Quarters					
	1	2	3	4	Total
Cornell	0	14	14	14	42
Penn	14	7	0	20	41

Scoring Summary

Penn –	Wilcox 7 pass from Becker (Loftus kick)
Penn –	Taylor 20 pass from Becker (Loftus kick)
Cornell –	Gellatly 25 pass from Mathews (Pierik kick)
Penn –	Elespuru 2 pass from Becker (Loftus kick)
Cornell –	Shapiro 4 pass from Mathews (Pierik kick)
Cornell –	Hagy 19 pass from Mathews (Pierik kick)
Cornell –	Avery – blocked punt in end zone (Pierik kick)
Cornell –	Mathews 1 run (Pierik kick)
Cornell –	Hagy 8 pass from Mathews (Pierik kick)
Penn –	Countryman 45 pass from Torgersen (Loftus kick)
Penn –	Taylor 25 pass from Torgersen (Loftus kick)
Penn –	Chwarzynski 39 interception return (kick blocked)

Attendance – 7,057

2013: Up and Down

At the end of this up-and-down season, in which the Quakers finished under .500 for the 1st time since 2007, head coach Al Bagnoli announced that 2014 would be his last year of coaching. (He later "un-retired," to become the head coach at Columbia). The team could never get untracked in 2014, and finished with a 2-8 overall record, the worst in Bagnoli's tenure. Bagnoli, whose overall record at Penn was 148-80 (65 percent wins), was replaced by **Ray Priore**, his long-time assistant. The future of the Quakers was in good hands.

58. *Block That Kick, Donald*

November 7, 2015 - Penn 26, Princeton 23 (OT)

"I just had to do it for everybody else."

Penn Wins Epic Overtime Affair

***Eric Fiore** (6) crosses the goal line to score the game-winning TD in overtime. The OT was made possible by Penn's **Donald Panciello**, who blocked a field goal at the end of regulation time.*

With Penn's Ivy League title hopes on the line, junior **Donald Panciello** blocked a field goal as time expired in regulation, sending the Franklin Field Homecoming crowd of 11,817 into a frenzy, and the Ivy League showdown with arch rival Princeton into overtime. Moments later, senior **Eric Fiore** caught an 11-yard touchdown pass to capture a dramatic 26-23 victory for the Quakers. Penn now controlled its own destiny toward a league-record 17th Ivy title - this wild win over Princeton set up a showdown with Harvard on the following Saturday, in Cambridge. And if all went as planned against the Crimson, they would be back in two weeks for a game against Cornell that would have the potential to conclude with another Ivy League title for the Red and Blue.

Penn trailed 20-10 at half-time, but held the Tigers scoreless in 2nd half. The Quakers tied the game on **Jimmy Gammill's** 42-yard field goal with 3:22 left, but Princeton drove right down to the Penn 25, and called timeout with only four seconds left. A blocked kick would have seemed improbable, had the Quakers not already done it - two years ago, in an Ivy matchup with Dartmouth (see pages 152-153), Penn blocked a field goal as time expired to send the game into overtime. That game, the longest in Ivy League history (4 overtimes), was also the last time Penn played past regulation.

The Penn faithful were hoping for a repeat of that day, when Princeton lined up for the game-winning, 35-yard field goal, and Panciello delivered. His rush off the edge caused the 1st missed field goal of the season for the Tigers in 11 attempts. "All of our guys work way too hard for our season to end right there. So I just had to do it for everybody else," said Panciello.

Princeton then got the ball 1st in overtime and threw three incompletions. This time, the field goal was good from 42 yards out for a 23-20 lead. But now Penn had the ball, and needed just three plays to win the game. After an incompletion, junior **Brian Schoenauer** ran for 14 yards. Fiore then corralled the game-winning toss from junior quarterback **Alek Torgersen**, scampered into the end zone, and set off a crazy celebration on the field and in the stands. "All I had to do was get it in his area and pray that he didn't miss the ball or that I overthrew it," Torgersen said of the walk off score.

The teams shared field goals in the 1st quarter, before Penn regained the lead with a 4-yard touchdown run from sophomore **Tre Solomon** at the 9:10 mark of the 2nd quarter. Princeton scored the last 17 points of the 1st half, however, tying the game on their next drive and then scoring again with 19 seconds remaining, for a 17-10 advantage. On the ensuing kickoff, the Quakers fumbled and Princeton recovered deep in Penn territory. That enabled the Tigers to tack on a field goal as time expired, for a 10-point lead at intermission.

Right after the break, Penn forced a punt and then drove 84 yards for a touchdown, with Solomon adding his 9th touchdown in the last four games - a 3-yard rush that pulled Penn within 20-17, with 5:57 left in the 3rd quarter. The Tigers then used up nearly eight minutes on a 19-play drive, but were stuffed on 4th-and-goal at the 1-yard line. Foreshadowing his late-game heroics, Panciello came off the edge to make the stop. Penn's offense then responded with a 95-yard drive, but that ended with a fumble inside the opponent's 5-yard line. The Quakers' defense came through though, with a three-and-out which set up Gammill's tying field goal in the 4th quarter.

Penn linebacker **Brandon Mills** had an outstanding game, as did Panciello, **Sam Philippi** and **Mason Williams**. Torgersen finished 21-of-27 for 178 yards and the game's final score, with sophomore wide receiver **Justin Watson** catching a career-high 13 of those 21 completions.

Score by Quarters						
	1	2	3	4	OT	Total
Princeton	3	17	0	0	3	23
Penn	3	7	7	3	6	26

Scoring Summary
Penn –   Gammill 27 FG
Princeton –   Bieck 43 FG
Penn –   Solomon 4 run (Gammill kick)
Princeton –   Rhattigan 4 run (Bieck kick)
Princeton –   Rhattigan 2 run (Bieck kick)
Princeton –   Bieck 39 FG
Penn –   Solomon 3 run (Gammill kick)
Penn –   Gammill 42 FG
Princeton –   Bieck 42 FG
Penn –   Fiore 11 pass from Torgersen
Attendance – 11,017

59. Quick Work

November 21, 2015 - Penn 34, Cornell 21

"To come out with two championships is special. Not a lot of people even get 1."

Quakers Make Quick Work of Big Red

Penn players celebrate winning Penn's 17th Ivy League championship, the 1st since 2012.

On Senior Day at Franklin Field, the Quakers defeated Cornell 34-21, to claim their 17th Ivy title, the 1st since 2012 and the 4th in seven years. Head Coach Ray Priore became just the 7th coach in league history to win an Ivy championship in his 1st season. He guided the Quakers to five straight wins to end the season - Penn's longest winning streak since 2010. In their final game in the Red and Blue, Penn's seniors celebrated their 2nd Ivy title, and became the 5th class in the last six years to graduate with at least two championship rings. "It's surreal. I don't know if it's hit me yet. I was trying to take it all in on the field. To come out with two championships is special. Not a lot of people even get 1," said Penn tight end **Ryan O'Malley**.

Making quick work of the task at hand, Penn scored on its 1st four possessions and never looked back. **Justin Watson** became just the 3rd player in school history with 1,000 career receiving yards in a season, and is the 3rd receiver in Ivy history with five straight 100-yard receiving games. He was the focus early, as his 33-yard reception in the game's 1st possession set up running back **Brian Schoenauer**'s 6-yard touchdown run, on an option pitch from quarterback **Alek Torgersen**. After an unsuccessful 2-point try, Penn led 6-0. The Penn defense followed the offense's impressive start with an interception on Cornell's 1st play from scrimmage. Defensive lineman **Austin Taps** deflected the pass, and it fluttered into the arms of linebacker **Brandon Mills**, setting the Quakers up at the Cornell 32.

Five plays later, Penn struck again, this time with a bit of trickery. Senior wide receiver **Eric Fiore** took a handoff and then threw a 14-yard touchdown pass to O'Malley in the back of the end zone. **Jimmy Gammill** connected on the extra point, and the Quakers led 13-0, less than five minutes into the contest. After a 3-and-out from the Penn defense, the offense went back to work with another touchdown drive. Torgersen delivered a 37-yard pass to Watson again, this time with Watson crossing the goal line, to put the Quakers on top, 20-0, with 7:40 left in the opening quarter. Cornell scored early in the 2nd quarter to make it 20-7, but **Lonnie Tuff** returned the ensuing kickoff 93 yards to the Cornell 4-yard line. Three plays later, Torgersen walked in for a 1-yard score, to push the lead to 27-7 at the half.

The Quakers continued their impressive offensive showing with a score on their 1st drive of the 2nd half, going 67 yards in 11 plays, and capping the drive with another touchdown pass from Torgersen to Watson. Cornell scored at the end of the 3rd quarter and with 1:11 remaining in the game to close the final margin to 34-21, but that score was not indicative of Penn's overall dominance of this contest. In Ray Priore's first year as head coach, another Ivy League championship was in the books for Penn.

Score by Quarters					
	1	2	3	4	Total
Cornell	0	7	7	7	21
Penn	20	7	7	0	34

Scoring Summary

Penn –	Schoenauer 6 run (run failed)
Penn –	O'Malley 14 pass from Fiore (Gammill kick)
Penn –	Watson 37 pass from Torgersen (Gammill kick)
Cornell –	Somborn 1 run (Mays kick)
Penn –	Torgersen 3 run (Gammill kick)
Penn –	Watson 12 pass from Torgersen (Gammill kick)
Cornell –	Hubbard 43 pass from Somborn (Mays kick)
Cornell –	Hagy 2 pass from Somborn (Mays kick)

Attendance – 6,007

2015: Change in "Priore-ties" A surprisingly lopsided loss to Lehigh in the season opener had Penn fans concerned about the new coaching regime. However, the following week the Quakers pulled off a shocking (24-13) upset of Villanova, *defeating the Wildcats for the 1st time in 104 years*, and on the 'Cats home field to boot. With quarterback **Alek Torgersen** passing and wide receiver **Justin Watson** catching, this team was an offensive juggernaut. After a loss to Dartmouth in its Ivy opener, Penn rolled to six straight Ivy wins and a tie for the title; thus, the class of 2016 became the 7th consecutive class to win at least one Ivy League championship.

60. Winning Is Elementary

October 29, 2016 – Penn 21, Brown 14

"It's elementary, my dear Watson."

Quakers Take Early Lead, Hold on for Victory

Justin Watson races down the sideline, en route to a 67-yard 1st-quarter touchdown.

For the better part of two seasons, **Justin Watson** had staked claim to being one of the best wide receivers in the storied history of Penn football. In front of a boisterous Homecoming crowd, Watson furthered his argument with a career high 210 yards on 11 catches, as the Quakers stayed perfect in the Ivy League with a 21-14 win over Brown. Watson's 210 yards were the 4th-most in a single game in program history, and he became the 1st Quaker to reach the 200-yard mark since **Dan Castles** against Cornell in 2003. The Bears had no answers for Watson in the 1st half, as he caught eight passes for 158 yards and a touchdown, helping Penn build a 21-0 half-time lead. Brown did not wilt, however, scoring twice in the 2nd half to close within one score. The Red and Blue would need a **Sam Philippi** interception in the end zone with 1:28 remaining in the game to secure the win, but the Quakers had now won 10 consecutive Ivy League games.

Penn's defense was up to its usual standards in the 1st half – shutting out the opponent for the 3rd consecutive week. **Nick Miller** led the way with eight tackles, while cornerback **Mason Williams** was in on 6, as Brown registered just 98 yards of total offense. Fueled by the defense, the Quakers' offense engineered three scoring drives to produce their 21-0 half-time margin. After Brown missed on a 34-yard field goal attempt midway through the 1st quarter, the Quakers hit the gas pedal and needed just three plays to take a 7-0 lead. QB **Alek Torgersen** ran for 13 yards, and on the next play hit Watson for a 67-yard touchdown – Penn's longest TD pass of the season. In the 2nd quarter, the Quakers took more of a methodical approach. A 15-play, 87-yard march down the field was capped off by a 17-yard touchdown pass from Torgersen to wide receiver **Christian Pearson**. Torgersen followed that up by leading Penn's longest scoring drive of the season to end the 1st half. With just 22 seconds left, **Tre Solomon** plunged in from one yard out to finish off a 16-play, 82-yard drive to paydirt.

Brown's offense finally sparked in the 3rd quarter following a Penn fumble, which yielded a short field for the Bears. five plays later, the Bears scored from 1-yard out for their 1st points of the day. Following two Penn punts, Brown once again cut into the lead. After a 58-yard pass completion, the Bears scored from the 2-yard line, making the score 21-14 heading into the final quarter. The Quakers had a chance to make the game a 2-score contest early in the 4th quarter, but a field-goal attempt went wide right with 6:57 remaining. Still clinging to life—down by just seven points—Brown drove the ball all the way to the Penn 28; however, Penn's defense responded from there. First, Miller and Williams tallied back-to-back tackles for losses, setting up 3rd-and-16 for Brown from the Penn 31. Philippi then took matters into his own hands, making the defensive play of the day with his interception in the end zone, and restoring respiration to the Penn fans.

Score by Quarters	1	2	3	4	Total
Brown	0	0	14	0	**14**
Penn	7	14	0	0	**21**

Scoring Summary

Penn – Watson 67 pass from Torgersen (Gammill kick)
Penn – Pearson 17 pass from Torgersen (Gammill kick)
Penn – Solomon 1 run (Gammill kick)
Brown – Linta 1 run (Goepferich kick)
Brown – Pena 2 run (Goepferich kick)
Attendance – 8,047

61. The Drive

November 11, 2016 - Penn 27, Harvard 14

"We had one last time to light up the Frank. I couldn't be any happier."

Long Drive Topples Crimson in Final Minute

Justin Watson celebrates his game-winning TD with less than one minute remaining.

On a night where he re-wrote the Penn record book, senior quarterback **Alek Torgersen** left a lasting memory with his final touchdown pass at Franklin Field – a 2-yard delivery to his favorite target with just 15 seconds to play, which secured a rousing Quaker win over Harvard. Torgersen found **Justin Watson** to cap a 10-play, 80-yard drive, which ended with Torgersen's 51st career touchdown pass – breaking the Penn record set by **Gavin Hoffman** (1999-2001). The Penn bench erupted in celebration after Torgersen's touchdown pass, and the party in the end zone was so good, the defense wanted in too. Harvard had 15 seconds to find a miracle, but instead found **Sam Philippi.** The sophomore safety forced a fumble, and **Tyler**

Hendrickson scooped it up and scored Penn's 2nd defensive touchdown of the night as time ran out, making the final score 27-14. Time had expired, so there was no extra point attempt. "We had one last time to light up the Frank. I couldn't be any happier," said Torgersen.

Penn's road to victory was slow in developing. On a 40-degree night, with winds gusting upwards of 25 mph, it seemed as if points would be at a premium. The Red and Blue struggled on offense for most of the game – Penn did not run a single play in Harvard territory in the 1st half – but were picked up by the defense, who dialed up a season-defining game. Penn's lone points of the 1st half came off a **Louis Vecchio** 40-yard interception return for a touchdown midway through the 2nd quarter, giving the Red and Blue a 7-3 lead.

In the 2nd half, the Quakers finally ran a play in Harvard territory – and it was a doozy. After a nine-yard **Tre Solomon** rush gave Penn 1st-and-10 from the Harvard 47, Torgersen connected with **Christian Pearson** on a 47-yard touchdown, to extend Penn's lead to 14-3, with 10:30 to play in the 3rd quarter. Vecchio and the defense would keep Harvard at bay for a while, conceding just a 25-yard field goal with 12:44 left, before a late Crimson rally almost forced overtime. With 5:51 to go, Harvard started at Penn's 38 after a 26-yard punt return. Eight plays later – including a nine-yard pass on 4th-and-7 from the Penn 35 – a 26-yard touchdown pass brought the Crimson to within two, 14-12. Harvard lined up for a 2-point conversion. The snap went directly to the Harvard running back, who reversed the ball to wide receiver Justice Shelton-Mosley, who tossed a pass to an open (quarterback) Joe Viviano to tie the game at 14-14. (Hmmm – sounds suspiciously like the "Philly Special").

With all three timeouts and 3:23 on the clock, Penn was undaunted, and thus began a drive, led by Torgersen, that will go down in Penn football history as one of the greatest ever. Harvard was offside on the kickoff, giving Penn a free five yards to start at its own 25. On his final drive on his home field, Torgersen was 8-for-10 for all 80 yards. He connected with three different receivers, with four passes going to

Watson, including the final one – the game-winner. Torgersen-to-Watson's 17 touchdowns now tied for the most by a Penn pair.

The Quakers hoped to close out their 2016 season with their 2nd consecutive Ivy League title, needing to defeat Cornell in Ithaca on the following Saturday to do so.

Score by Quarters

	1	2	3	4	Total
Harvard	3	0	0	11	14
Penn	0	7	7	13	27

Scoring Summary
Harvard –   McIntyre 20 FG
Penn –   Vecchio 40 interception return (Gammill kick)
Penn –   Pearson 47 pass from Torgersen (Gammill kick)
Harvard –   McIntyre 25 FG
Harvard –   Foster 26 pass from Viviano (Viviano pass from Shelton-Mosley)
Penn –   Watson 2 pass from Torgersen (Gammill kick)
Penn –   Hendrickson 18 fumble recovery
Attendance – 5,092

2016: Torgersen to Watson – A Winning Combo
Following the above dramatic last-second victory against Harvard, the following week the Quakers clinched a tie for their 18th Ivy League title, with a smashing (42-20) victory over Cornell, in the season finale in Ithaca. As occurred all season, the passing combination of Alek Torgersen to Justin Watson lit up the opposing (in this case – Cornell) defense. The senior quarterback finished 24 of 31 passing for 284 yards and a TD, and added 58 yards and a TD rushing. The junior wide receiver caught 11 passes for 106 yards, becoming Penn's all-time single-season leader in receptions and receiving yards. "It was a great day to be a Quaker" said coach Priore.

Franklin Field Saturdays

62. Will to Win

November 4, 2017 - Penn 38, Princeton 35

"We had total confidence in Will leading us down there on that final drive."

Quakers' 'Will' to Win Shocks Tigers

Penn's **Louis Vecchio** celebrates the Quakers' win versus Princeton.

The Penn and Princeton football teams met for the 109th time on this Franklin Field Saturday, and in the highest-scoring game in this rivalry since 1940, the Quakers prevailed, 38-35. When the game was over, the Homecoming crowd of 9,073 was walking out of Franklin Field with nearly as many talking points as there were combined yards in the contest.

It was a game Penn people won't forget, or stop talking about, for a long time. The final scoring of the day came with just 1:12 remaining, when quarterback **Will Fischer-Colbrie** found his All-American wide receiver, **Justin Watson,** for a 15-yard touchdown. It was the last of eight catches for Watson, on a day when he became the program's all-time leader in career receptions and added to his records for career receiving yards and receiving touchdowns. **Jack Soslow** nailed the PAT, and that set the score at Penn 38, Princeton 35. Penn's kickoff was a touchback, so Princeton started on its own 20. After two false-start penalties, Princeton quarterback Chad Kanoff then threw a pass to Jesper Horsted that was tipped and picked off by **Jyron Walker**. Game over, right?

Nope, not yet. Penn was called for offsides, and the next thing the crowd knew, Princeton had driven down the field to the Penn 13-yard line. On 2nd and 5, and with 12 seconds left, Kanoff sent a pass into the deep right corner of the end zone that Stephen Carlson appeared to bobble and then catch. Immediately, the referee on the sideline signaled touchdown and the Princeton bench went crazy.

Wait - hold on. The referee on the back line ran in and signaled 'no catch.' After a discussion, and despite massive protestations from the Tigers sideline, <u>that</u> call (no catch) remained. Princeton still had seven seconds left, though, and since it was 3rd down, the Tigers decided to attempt a 31-yard field goal and send the game to overtime. two Penn timeouts later, the ball was snapped and the ball was kicked... Wide right. Pandemonium switched sidelines, the Quakers players bouncing all over the place and being held back by the coaches lest they get called for a delay-of-game penalty (3 seconds still remained). Order was finally restored, Fischer-Colbrie took a knee, and NOW the game was really over. "We had total confidence in Will leading us down there on that final drive. It's awesome to see all the work he put in these last couple of years paying off for him," said Justin Watson.

It was a game Princeton people won't forget, or stop talking about for a long time, either. Here's why: Punishing the Tigers with its running attack, led by **Abe Willows**, Penn took a 17-7 lead in the 2nd quarter, with that score holding up at half-time. Penn had the 1st possession of the 2nd half, and the Quakers took advantage with their 3rd touchdown of the day, a spectacular 36-yard pass play from Fischer - Colbrie to Watson, who somehow caught the ball in stride and kept his feet in, and put Penn up, 24-7. However, Penn essentially gifted Princeton the next 14 points to make this a game. After the 2nd touchdown, Penn's lead was down to a nervous 24-21, as the teams entered the final quarter.

Penn scored again to restore some semblance of order, but that also came with a measure of controversy. **Tre Solomon** broke free and suddenly was in the open, running across the field for a sure touchdown. However, as he got to the 5-yard line Solomon raised the ball in triumph before hitting the end zone, and was flagged for unsportsmanlike conduct. Instead of an easy score, Penn was marched back to the Princeton 20. Fortunately for Solomon, four plays later the Red and Blue were back in the end zone, as **Karekin Brooks** punched it in. 31-21 Penn.

Princeton's offense was clicking by this time, however, and the Tigers marched right down the field for their 3rd score in as many drives. The score now was 31-28 Penn, with 8:47 to play. Penn fumbled another exchange near midfield, and once again Princeton came up with the football. Starting in Quakers territory once again, the Tigers took advantage and went up by 35-31 with a 5-play drive.

Penn, victimized by late scores this season, could have wilted. Instead, the offense went out and put together a gutsy, 80-yard drive that ended with Justin Watson's aforementioned final, game-winning catch in the end zone.

Yes, it was a game people won't forget, or stop talking about, for a long time. On either side.

Score by Quarters	1	2	3	4	Total
Princeton	7	0	14	14	**35**
Penn	7	10	7	14	**38**

Scoring Summary

Princeton –	Carlson 22 pass from Kanoff (Rice kick)
Penn -	Willows 1 run (Soslow kick)
Penn -	Soslow 34 FG
Penn -	Willows 12 run (Soslow kick)
Penn -	Watson 36 pass from Fischer-Colbrie (Soslow kick)
Princeton -	Horsted 17 pass from Kanoff (Rice kick)
Princeton -	Horsted 9 pass from Kanoff (Rice kick)
Penn -	Brooks 2 run (Soslow kick)
Princeton -	Volker 1 run (Rice kick)
Princeton -	Volker 3 run (Rice kick)
Penn -	Watson 15 pass from Fischer-Colbrie (Soslow kick)

Attendance – 9,073

63. The Greatest

November 18, 2017 - Penn 29, Cornell 22

"Hopefully, we'll be watching him (Justin Watson) on Sundays soon."

Quakers' Watson Keys Thrilling Win

Justin Watson *(5) beams with pride while holding the Trustees' Cup in his hands, after a game in which he solidified his place as the best wide receiver in Penn history. Looking on in the "top row" (wearing a cap) is **Vhito Decapria**, honorary team captain.*

> *"Down the stretch, he might have touched the ball every play. I don't know very many people in our league, or in the FCS, that can make some of the catches he made in this game."*
> David Archer, Cornell head coach, re Justin Watson.

In a fitting end to a season which tested every ounce of their grit, the Quakers banded together to make one final goal-line stand on the game's final play, holding on for a 29-22 victory over the Big Red. With the win, they finished 2017 on a four-game winning streak, for a 4-3 mark in Ivy League play. Those three losses came by a combined 11 points. All three had come with under five minutes to play, with two of them being dealt on the game's final play – including the Ivy opener, in which Dartmouth scored on 4th-and-goal from the 1-yard line with no time remaining.

In this game, after a 28-yard completion from quarterback Dalton Banks to receiver Collin Shaw, Cornell had a 1st-and-goal with 18 seconds left. The next play was a rush over the top, which was stuffed by the Quakers tackle **Nick Miller.** The clock nearly ran out, but Banks spiked the ball just before the clock expired, and the referees properly reset the time to 0:01. Given another chance, Banks rolled out to his right, but **Jacob Martin** knocked down his pass into the end zone, securing a thrilling win (and the 2017 Trustees' Cup), and sending the Class of 2018 off riding high.

Quite a bit of drama had preceded the above gut-wrenching finish. After a 21-10 lead at half-time, Penn watched the Big Red score the game's next 12 points--via two touchdowns and two failed two-point conversions--to take a 22-21 lead early in the 4th quarter. The Quakers were still trailing by the same score with 8:21 to play in the game, as they stepped to the line for what would be their final drive of the season. That would be their own *3*-yard line. And a new quarterback was under center.

Nick Robinson took over and went 5-for-7 for 75 yards, driving the Quakers down the field to take the lead. He almost covered all 97 yards in one play, when he found **Nicholas Bokun** free behind the Cornell defense on second-and-10 from the 3, but the ball just slipped out of Bokun's hands as he tried to catch it in stride. No worries. Bokun redeemed himself with a 13-yard catch on a 3rd-and-9 later in the drive.

On 3rd down after the Bokun miss, Robinson made the right read – find **Justin Watson** – and the All-American hauled in a 13-yard catch to extend the drive. It was one of three catches for Watson on the drive – but not the biggest. On 3rd-and-1 from the Cornell 37, he chased down a Robinson heave and dove to make perhaps the most spectacular of his Penn-record 286 career catches. He had corralled the ball at the Cornell 3, and on the next play, **Tre Solomon** barreled in to give Penn a 27-22 lead. The Quakers elected to go for 2, and Robinson passed to

Watson, who plowed into the end zone to make the score 29-22, with 2:06 left. Cornell still had some fight left in them, however, and as described above, put a scare into the Quakers and their fans, until Jacob Martin's (and the rest of the defense's) heroics saved the day.

Score by Quarters					
	1	2	3	4	Total
Cornell	10	0	6	6	22
Penn	7	14	0	8	29

Scoring Summary
Cornell –   Null 32 FG
Penn -   Brooks 38 run (Soslow kick)
Cornell -   Shaw 35 pass from Banks (Null kick)
Penn -   Brooks 6 run (Soslow kick)
Penn -   Watson 22 pass from Fischer-Colbrie (Soslow kick)
Cornell -   Pope 3 run (pass failed)
Cornell -   Banks 1 run (pass failed)
Penn -   Solomon 3 run (Watson pass from Robinson)
Attendance – 3,861

2017: The "G.O.A.T.'s" Last Season

Justin Watson (now playing for the Tampa Bay Buccaneers) finished his career at Penn with several school career records, including, but not limited to: receptions (286), receiving yards (3,777), receiving touchdowns (33), all-purpose yards (4,116) and touchdowns in a season (14 in 2017), and walked off of Franklin Field a winner in his career finale. "It's been a blessing," said Penn's greatest wide receiver ever. "Penn and this football team has given me so much. I'm just so happy I've been able to give back to this program for everything they've given to me." Without Watson in 2018, the Quakers would finish at 6-4 overall and 3-4 in the Ivy, good for 4th place.

64. Nail-Biter

November 2, 2019 - Penn 38, Brown 36

"That's the best feeling in the world, with all of the work you put in going in to that kick."

Last-Second Field Goal Saves Quakers

*Penn's **Daniel Karrash** (94) celebrates his winning field goal with holder **Kolton Huber** (10).*

The Penn team got its 1st Ivy League win of 2019 in dramatic fashion on this Franklin Field Saturday, as **Daniel Karrash** kicked a 22-yard field goal—his 1st attempt as a collegian—with just two seconds left, to give the Quakers a 38-36 win over Brown. Karrash's kick, which he acknowledged was the 1st walk-off winner of his career, was an exclamation point on a defining drive when Penn needed it most.

The Quakers' offense had essentially been shut down the entire 2nd half, its only touchdown coming on a 1-play drive after the defense had gifted them with an interception. Brown, meanwhile, had made up a 16-point deficit to take a 36-35 lead with 4:10 left in the game. Now down by a point, Penn embarked on a drive that wound up being 16 plays—6 more than the Quakers had run in its previous five drives during the half, and covering 74 yards. It brought the Red and Blue all the way down to Brown's 1-yard line, before quarterback **Nick Robinson** took a snap on the right hash and took a knee in the middle of the field at the 6. With five seconds left, the game was on Karrash's foot and he went right down the middle with his kick. "That's the best feeling in the world, with all of the work you put in going in to that kick. I feel like everybody put in too much work for me to miss that," said Karrash.

Penn still had to kick off after the field goal. After Brown's returner took a knee, the Bears attempted a final pass, but **Brian O'Neill**, the Quaker defensive hero of the day, intercepted it. Thus Penn got the win, in a game in which Brown ran 94 plays to Penn's 62, and outgained the Quakers in yardage by 477-304.

Penn held a 21-19 lead at half-time, thanks to two short touchdown runs by **Abe Willows** and a 24-yard TD pass from **Nick Robinson** to **Ryan Cragun**. Brown started the 2nd half with the ball, but on the Bears' 3rd play O'Neill picked off a pass at Brown's 29 and a returned it to the 11. Robinson hit **Rory Starkey** on the next play for a TD, and just one minute into the period it was 28-19. Exactly one minute after that, O'Neill recovered a Bear fumble and returned it 21 yards to the end zone, for a 35-19 Quakers lead. At that point in the game, it looked like Penn could put things on cruise control, but that proved to be a mirage.

A 24-yard field goal by Brown made it 35-22, then it was 35-29 with 13:09 left, when Allen Smith ran it in from one yard out, capping an 11-play, 47-yard drive. Penn returned the ensuing kickoff for a touchdown, but a hold was called, and instead the Quakers started deep in their own territory and went 3-and-out. Brown got the ball on the Penn side of midfield and rolled downhill to the end zone against a gassed Penn defense. The Bears needed eight plays to score, with quarterback E. J. Perry scoring on a 16-yard scamper around the right side on 4th-and-3.

Penn could have used a sustained drive after that. Robinson tried to hit

Cragun for a long strike, but Brown easily intercepted it near midfield. However, the Penn defense held on 4th-and-10, and that set the stage for the Red and Blue's winning drive. "That's life, right?" Penn coach Ray Priore said. "You have those highs and you get down to the lows. You just have to keep on swinging and don't stop."

Score by Quarters					
	1	2	3	4	Total
Brown	7	12	3	14	**36**
Penn	0	21	14	3	**38**

Scoring Summary
Brown –   Perry 50 run (Goepferich kick)
Penn –   Willows 1 run (Karrash kick)
Penn –   Willows 8 run (Karrash kick)
Brown –   Perry 3 run (kick failed)
Penn –   Cragun 24 pass from Robinson (Karrash kick)
Brown –   Prall 37 pass from Perry (pass failed)
Penn –   Starkey 11 pass from Robinson (Karrash kick)
Penn –   O'Neill 21 fumble recovery (Karrash kick)
Brown –   Goepferich 24 FG
Brown –   Smith 1 run (Goepferich kick)
Brown –   Perry 16 run (Goepferich kick)
Penn –   Karrash 22 FG
Attendance – 8,459

65. Razzle Dazzle

November 9, 2019 – Penn 21 Cornell 20

"Give 'em the old razzle dazzle."

Quakers Stop Two Pointer at Finish, After "Razzle Dazzle" Play Puts Them Ahead

*Senior defensive lineman **Prince Emili** (78) exhorts the Penn defense near the end of the game.*

> *"On that play, he just caught the ball, snapped it and threw it, like a 2nd baseman."*
> **Ray Priore**, Penn head coach

Good luck finding anyone at Franklin Field who foresaw Penn's eventual game-winning touchdown coming off a play started in the hands of the backup quarterback, who threw back to a transfer quarterback/returner/receiver, who then uncorked an 80-yard touchdown pass to a converted defensive back who'd never before caught a touchdown. But that's just what the Quakers dialed up with 13:21 remaining in the 4th quarter, as **Ryan Glover** tossed a screen pass to **Owen Goldsberry**, who then launched a perfect arc to **Eric Markes** to put the Quakers ahead by 21-14 over Cornell.

As exciting as it was, that play didn't end the game. Cornell rallied, and capped a 16-play, 94-yard drive with a 10-yard TD pass from quarterback Richie Kenney to Phazione McClurge with 50 seconds remaining in regulation. The Big Red left the offense on the field to go for 2, but Penn freshman cornerback **Kendren Smith** stepped in to knock down a Kenney pass attempt and keep the Quakers in the lead. Then, Penn suffered through two onside kick attempts. The 1st of these was ruled to have gone out of bounds, but (fortunately) for the Big Red though – they'd gone offside on the play and had to re-kick. This time, **Ryan Cragun** batted the kick out of bounds and the Quakers could celebrate a homecoming win and retaining the Trustees' Cup.

The game wasn't pretty, but it sure was exciting, despite both teams' offenses taking time to find their mojos. Penn scored 1st, early in the 2nd quarter. On 3rd-and-9 from the Cornell 12, **Nick Robinson** connected with **Rory Starkey, Jr.** for a diving catch which put Penn on the board. The Big Red answered midway through the 2nd quarter, needing three plays to level the game at 7-7, on a 45-yard TD pass. The score remained tied at half-time.

Midway through the 3rd quarter, Cornell took a 14-7 lead, following an 11-play, 80-yard drive. At that point, Glover took over at quarterback for Penn, and he led a 4-play, 75-yard TD drive, which needed just 1:44 to complete. Glover opened with a 20-yard screen to **Karekin Brooks**, then three plays later uncorked a jump pass to **Kolton Huber,** who hauled it in for a 40-yard touchdown catch to tie the score at 14-14, with 3:12 left in the 3rd. After halting Cornell's next drive, Penn needed just two plays to take the lead. The 1st was a screen pass to Goldsberry which gained just two yards. The 2nd started out the same way – a screen to Goldsberry – but then came the "razzle dazzle," as the transfer from Michigan who started the year as a quarterback showed why he did so, by making his 1st career touchdown pass.

Penn head coach Ray Priore heaped praise on Goldsberry for making the right read. "He went to Michigan as a walk-on and played wide receiver," Priore said. On that play, he just caught the ball, snapped it and threw it, like a 2nd baseman in baseball. He's a terrific athlete and is so football-smart."

After that big play, the Big Red temporarily seemed off kilter. However they did not wilt, marching 94 yards over 16 plays before Kenney found McClurge to close within one and set up the deciding 2-point play. "It's our mentality and heart," senior defensive lineman **Prince Emili** said of the overall defensive effort, especially on the deciding 2-point conversion attempt. Another exciting and successful Franklin Field Saturday had come to a close.

Score by Quarters					
	1	2	3	4	Total
Cornell	0	7	7	6	**20**
Penn	0	7	7	7	**21**

Scoring Summary
Penn –   Starkey 12 pass from Robinson (Karrash kick)
Cornell –   McClurge 45 pass from Kenney (Null kick)
Cornell –   Harrell 1 run (Null kick)
Penn –   Huber 40 pass from Glover (Karrash kick)
Penn –   Markes 80 pass from Goldsberry (Karrash kick)
Cornell –   McClurge 10 pass from Kenney (pass failed)
Attendance – 11,487

2019: Hanging in There
After the above exciting victory over Cornell, the Quakers traveled up to Harvard, where they prevailed by 24-20, on a 4th-quarter, 16-yard TD pass from Nick Robinson to Cory Starkey. In the season finale against the eventual 2019 Ivy champion Princeton at Franklin Field, the Red and Blue hung in for a half, but ultimately lost to the superior Tiger team. 18 points in the 2nd half secured a 28-7 Princeton victory. Another season of football at Franklin Field had come to a close. Little did anyone know what was about to happen in 2020.

Wait 'Till Next Year

July 8, 2020 – Season Cancelled

"This too, shall pass."

Covid Causes Cancellation of All Ivy Athletics Until 2021

*An empty **Franklin Field** tells the story, as the Ivy League cancelled its 2020 football season because of the Coronavirus pandemic.*

On July 8, 2020, the Ivy League announced that due to the Coronavirus pandemic, it had cancelled all competitive sports at least until January 1, 2021, making it the 1st NCAA Division I athletic conference to enact such a policy.

On November 12, 2020, the League further announced that it would not conduct competition for Winter sports during the 2020-21 season either, nor would it conduct competition for Fall 2020 sports during the upcoming spring semester. Then, in February 2021, the League announced that intercollegiate athletics competition for Spring sports was also cancelled.

2021: Update – Good News:
As of this writing, thankfully the 2021 football season is "on." After two non-league road games on September 18 and September 25, football will return once again to Franklin Field on *Friday* evening October 1, for Penn's Ivy League opener versus Dartmouth.

"Hail! Pennsylvania, through endless days."

Bibliography/Sources

Books
1. Goldstein, John. *Ivy League Autumns*. New York: St Martin's Press, 1996.
2. McCallum, John D. *Ivy League Football Since 1872*. Briarcliff Manor, NY: Stein and Day, 1977.
3. Rottenberg, Dan. *Fight On, Pennsylvania*. Philadelphia: University of Pennsylvania Press, 1985.
4. University of Pennsylvania, *Class of 1960 "Record"* (Yearbook), 1960.

Articles
Sources for each game
Game #/Year/Opponent:
1. 1956 Dartmouth:
    Daily Pennsylvanian Archives ('DP'): 10/8/56 Article by Dan Dawley (excerpts); Photos (page 10) by George Satterthwaite. Penn Archives: Photo (page 7) – courtesy of "Fight On, Pennsylvania," by Dan Rottenberg (1985).
2. 1957 Yale:
    DP: 11/12/57 Article "Four Gridders Selected Stars" (excerpts). Penn Archives: Photos - courtesy of "Fight On, Pennsylvania."
3. 1958 Brown:
    DP: 10/20/58 Article by Edward Coplon (excerpts); Photos by Josh Pober (page 14) & Charles Hansing (page 16).
4. 1959 Dartmouth:
    DP: 10/6/59 Articles by Alfred Haber (excerpts) & William Bates (in entirety).
    1960 University of Pennsylvania Yearbook ("Record"): Photo.
5. 1959 Yale:
    DP: 11/10/59 Articles by Stephen Weiss (excerpts) & William Bates (in entirety).
    1960 "Record": Photos.
6. 1959 Cornell:

DP: 12/1/59 Article by Alfred Haber (in entirety); Photo (page 24) by Nelson Cohen.
1960 "Record": Photos (page 27).
7. 1963 Harvard:
DP: 11/4/63 Articles by Alan Richman (excerpts), Robert Style (excerpts), & Dan Rottenberg (in entirety); Photo by Richard Halperin.
8. 1965 Harvard:
DP: 11/1/65 Article by Guy Blynn (excerpts); Photo by David Hardman.
9. 1965 Columbia:
DP: 11/15/65 Article by Dave Sachsman (excerpts); Photo by David Hardman.
10. 1968 Princeton:
DP: 10/28/68 Article by Al Baden (excerpts); Photos (page 41) by Ken Souser.
Penn Archives: Photo (page 43) - courtesy "Fight On, Pennsylvania."
11. 1968 Dartmouth:
DP: 11/25/68 Articles by Howard Topel & Barry Jordan (excerpts); Photo by Jeff Sterling.
12. 1969 Brown:
DP:10/6/69 Article by Ira Garr (excerpts); Photo by Gary Cowen.
13. 1970 Princeton:
DP: 10/26/70 Article by John Wertheimer (excerpts); Photo by George Bloom.
14. 1971 Harvard:
DP: 11/1/71 Article by Tony Kovatch (excerpts); Photo by Nathan Sturman.
15. 1972 Princeton:
DP: 10/30/72 Article by Glenn Unterberger (excerpts); Photo by Ed Roth.
16. 1972 Yale:
DP: 11/13/72 Article by Glenn Unterberger (excerpts); Photo by Bob Shasha.
17. 1972 Dartmouth:
DP: 11/28/72 Articles by Dave Chandler (excerpts) & Phil Shimkin (entirety); Photo by Ed Roth.

18. 1973 Harvard:
    DP: 11/5/73 Article by Buzz Bissinger (excerpts); Photo by Mike Leibowitz.
19. 1973 Cornell:
    DP: 11/27/73 Article by Buzz Bissinger (excerpts); Photo by Joe Steinfeld.
20. 1974 Princeton:
    DP: 10/28/74 Article by Ed Wiest (excerpts); Photo by Joe Steinfeld.
21. 1975 Cornell:
    DP: 11/24/75 Article by Paul Burger (excerpts); Photo by Peter Grant.
22. 1977 Princeton:
    DP: 10/31/77 Article by Andy Rose (excerpts); Photo by Bruce Rosenbloom.
23. 1980 Columbia:
    DP: 10/6/80 Article by David Elfin (excerpts); Photo by Michael Speirs.
24. 1981 Cornell:
    DP: 9/21/81 Article by Bryan Harris (excerpts); Photos by Ken Platt (page 90) & Michael Eisenberg (page 93).
25. 1982 Yale:
    DP: 10/25/82 Article by Dave Zalesne (excerpts); Photo by Stephen Haymen.
26. 1982 Harvard:
    DP: 11/15/82 Articles by Dave Zalesne (excerpts); Photos by Barry Freedman (page 99 – top) & Steven Siegel (page 102).
    Franklin Field Illustrated 11/13/82/University of Pennsylvania - Cover Drawing (page 98) - artist unknown.
    Penn Archives: Photo (page 99 – bottom) courtesy of "Fight On, Pennsylvania."
    "Miracle On 33rd St - A Condensed Version" courtesy of Brian Gilmore (1982).
27. 1983 Princeton:
    "Fight On, Pennsylvania," (excerpts); Photo courtesy of same.
28. 1983 Dartmouth:
    DP: 11/21/83 Article by Ken Rosenthal (excerpts); Photo by Steven Siegel.

29. 1984 Harvard:
   DP: 11/12/84 Article by Bob Rifkin (excerpts); Photo (page 113) by Tom Leonardi; Photos (page 116) by Tom Leonardi, Dan Schmetter, Adam Gordon, Scott Langston.
30. 1985 Princeton:
   DP: 11/4/85 Article by David Goldberg (excerpts); Photo by Tom Leonardi.
31. 1985 Dartmouth:
   DP: 11/25/85 Article by Steve Goldwyn (excerpts); Photo by Tom Leonardi.
32. 1986 Harvard:
   DP: 11/17/86 Article by Dan Bollerman (excerpts); Photo by Tom Leonardi.
33. 1987 Brown:
   DP: 10/12/87 Article by Dan Bollerman (excerpts); Photo by Tom Leonardi.
34. 1988 Harvard:
   DP: 11/14/88 Article by Mike Finkel (excerpts); Photo by David Boretz.

35. 1992 Yale:
   DP: 11/2/92 Article by Eric Gomberg (excerpts); Photo by Paul Hu.
36. 1993 Dartmouth:
   DP: 9/20/93 Articles by Gabe Tsui (excerpts), Adam Steinmetz (in entirety); Photo by Marc Blumberg.
37. 1993 Princeton:
   DP: 11/8/93 Article by Michael Lief (excerpts); Photo by Asushi Egami.
38. 1993 Cornell:
   DP: 11/22/93 Article by Adam Steinmetz (excerpts); Photos by Sarit Zadok (page 149) & Eli Massa (page 152).
39. 1994 Harvard:
   DP: 11/14/94 Articles by Nicholas Hut (excerpts) & Adam Rubin (entirety); Photo by Zarit Sadok.
40. 1995 Princeton:
   DP: 11/6/95 Article by Srikaneth Reddy (excerpts); Photo by Stephen Shapiro.

41. 1997 Princeton:
   DP: 11/10/97 Article by Marc Chodock (excerpts); Photos by Karen Yiu (page 163) & Pelopidas Nicolaides (page 166).
42. 1998 Harvard:
   DP: 11/16/98 Article by Marc Chodock (excerpts); Photo by Matt Samuelowitz.
43. 2000 Brown:
   DP: 10/30/00 Article by Kyle Bahr (excerpts); Photo by David Graff.
44. 2000 Harvard:
   DP: 11/13/00 Article by Brian Hindo (excerpts); Photo by Michael Weissman.
45. 2002 Harvard:
   pennathletics.com: 11/9/17 Article "Pure Dominance" (excerpts of reprint of article written for the Daily Pennsylvanian in 2002, by David Zeitlin).
   Franklin Field Illustrated 10/13/12/University of Pennsylvania – Photo courtesy of same.
46. 2003 Yale:
   pennathletics.com: 10/25/03 Article (excerpts).
   Franklin Field Illustrated 10/2/04/University of Pennsylvania – Photo courtesy of same.
47. 2003 Cornell:
   pennathletics.com: 11/22/03 Article (excerpts).
   Franklin Field Illustrated 10/2/04/University of Pennsylvania – Photo page 185 courtesy of same.   Photo page 188 courtesy of Jake Perskie.
48. 2004 Brown:
   pennathletics.com: 10/30/04 Article by Mat Kanan (excerpts); Photo.
49. 2007 Yale:
   pennathletics.com: 10/20/07 Article (excerpts).
   Penn Archives/upenn.edu: Internet photo.
50. 2009 Princeton:
   pennathletics.com: 11/11/09 Article (excerpts); Photo.
51. 2009 Cornell:
   pennathletics.com: 11/21/09 Article (excerpts).
   alumni.upenn.edu: Internet image.

52. 2010 Dartmouth:
    pennathletics.com: 10/2/10 Article (excerpts); Photo.
53. 2010 Harvard:
    pennathletics.com: 11/13/10 Article (excerpts).
    Penn Archives/upenn.edu: Internet photo.
54. 2012 Columbia:
    pennathletics.com: 10/13/12 Article (excerpts).
    Franklin Field Illustrated 10/13/12/University of Pennsylvania: Photo courtesy of same.
55. 2012 Harvard:
    pennathletics.com: 11/10/12 Article (excerpts); Photo.
56. 2013 Dartmouth:
    pennathletics.com: 10/5/13 Article by Mike Mahoney (excerpts).
    Franklin Field Illustrated 10/26/13/University of Pennsylvania: Photo (courtesy of Drew Hallowell/Don Felice).
57. 2013 Cornell:
    pennathletics.com: 11/23/13 Article (excerpts).
    Penn Archives/upenn.edu: Photo.
58. 2015 Princeton:
    pennathletics.com: 11/7/15 Article (excerpts); Photo.
59. 2015 Cornell:
    pennathletics.com: 11/21/15 Article (excerpts); Photo.
60. 2016 Brown:
    pennathletics.com: 10/29/16 Article (excerpts); Photo.
61. 2016 Harvard:
    pennathletics.com: 11/11/16 Article (excerpts); Photo.
62. 2017 Princeton:
    pennathletics.com: 11/4/17 Article (excerpts), Photo.
63. 2017 Cornell:
    pennathletics.com: 11/18/17 Article (excerpts); Photo by Jon Kolbe.
64. 2019 Brown:
    pennathletics.com: 11/2/19 Article (excerpts); Photo by Hunter Martin Photography.
65. 2019 Cornell:
    pennathletics.com: 11/9/19 Article (excerpts); Photo by Mike Corsey.

2020 – "Wait 'Till Next Year":
www.penn.edu/Penn Archives: Internet photo.

About the Author:

Ted Gilmore is retired, after working for 40+ years in the Insurance industry, where he specialized in Workers' Compensation.

As part of a three-generational Penn family, Ted began attending Penn football games at Franklin Field when he was eight years old, and has rarely missed a game there since then - except during the 1980s, when his two children were involved in sports. The Pandemic of 2020 provided Ted with an opportunity to fulfill a goal of his - to put together a book about the best games played at Franklin Field since Penn joined the Ivy League in 1956. Producing this book also reduced his level of "withdrawal" resulting from the cancellation of Penn's 2020 football season.

A native Philadelphian, Ted is a graduate of Central High School (of Philadelphia) and Penn. He now lives in Willistown PA with his wife, Marygrace, with whom he recently celebrated Anniversary #50. When not attending Penn football games at Franklin Field (or Penn basketball games at the Palestra), he spends as much time as possible with his five grandchildren. This is his 1st book.

www.ingramcontent.com/pod-product-compliance
Lightning Source LLC
LaVergne TN
LVHW051545070426
835507LV00021B/2424